MW01503738

Complete
not lacking
full
whole
entire
total
unimpaired
undivided
flawless
impeccant
pure

Pray to
see converts
before God
me + other
people

Misc P131

Psalm 46:1 God is our
refuge and strength, a very present
help in trouble

God is all. God is my refuge for fear,
lonely, loneliness, restlessness, sadness. God,
not the problem, because the answer of
every thought + prayer

NORMAL CLASS NOTES
OF 1937

Oh every treatut
care, law pubstau

Normal Class Notes
of 1937

as taught by

Bicknell Young

The Bookmark
Santa Clarita, California

Young, Bicknell.
    Normal class notes / as taught by Bicknell Young
    p. cm.
    LCCN 2003104285
    ISBN 0-930227-54-9

    1. Spiritual healing. 2. Christian Science.
    3. Prayer—Christianity.   I. Title.

BX6950.Y68 2003   289.5
                           QB133-1289

Published by
The Bookmark
Post Office Box 801143
Santa Clarita, California 91380

CONTENTS

PUBLISHER'S FOREWORD

Volumes have been written on Christian Science since its discovery in 1866. Time has sifted these works, and preserved the best of them. *Notes from the Normal Class of 1937* is one of the classics. It was taught by Bicknell Young, then known as the Dean of Christian Science Teachers. His understanding of Christian Science went beyond mere theory, for he explained how to utilize its healing power, how to make it practical. These Class Notes represent some of his most profound teachings.

Normal Class Instruction

The purpose of the Normal Class was to prepare Christian Science practitioners to teach Christian Science. At the turn of the century when Mary Baker Eddy was organizing the Christian Science Church in Boston, Massachusetts, she established the Board of Education. Once every three years, the Board holds one class which lasts a week. It is known as the Normal Class. Thirty practitioners from all parts of the world come to Boston to be taught by a Christian Scientist experienced in healing and teaching. After a week's instruction, these practitioners become teachers and return to their local areas to teach Christian Science to others. Those selected are required to "have practised Christian Science healing successfully three years and . . . furnish evidence of their eligibility . . . All members of this class must be thorough English scholars." (*Church Manual*) It is considered an honor to be selected for the Normal Class, and a great honor to be asked to teach it.

Mrs. Eddy designated it a Normal Class because she did not intend it to be a long-term education in advanced metaphysics. The word *normal* in no way denotes advanced training or higher education. During the 1800's, the Normal Schools trained qualified persons to teach in the first grammar schools opening in the United States. This explains Mrs. Eddy's use of the word *normal* in connection with classes that were intended to train teachers in Christian Science.

When the Notes of the 1937 Normal Class were first recorded, they could not be circulated openly, for they could easily have been misunderstood. For many years, the notes were shared secretly among the more advanced students in the Church. The notes were so rare at one time as to command $150.00 for a single copy. But times have changed. World thought is rapidly shifting from physics to metaphysics. We live in a mental age, and are learning the subjective nature of all things. And so it seems only right that the 1937 Notes be made available to anyone seeking a better understanding of Christian Science.

Mr. Young was one of the early Scientists who understood so clearly mental cause and effect. For this reason, his teachings seem even more relevant to the present mental climate then when he first gave them to his students. As our world moves deeper into a mental age, the writings of such thinkers are coming into their own, for they explain the subjective nature of reality. They carry metaphysics beyond the mental plane into the spiritual realm, making them divine metaphysics, or Christian Science.

The Church Then and Now

In these notes, Mr. Young says a great deal about the Christian Science Church and Sunday School. In 1937 Christian Science churches throughout the world were flourishing, healing work was prolific, and the movement was at its peak. After World War II, the Church began to decline, until today it is a mere shadow of former years. This decline is due in large measure to the fact that the Church organization in Boston does not make available the deeper metaphysics upon which the progress of the Christian Science movement depends. The Christian Science periodicals have become tools mainly for promoting the views of the organization. The pure metaphysics taught by Mrs. Eddy and her students have been diluted into a form of modern day inspirational writing that bears little resemblance to Christian Science as expressed in such works as the *Normal Class Notes of 1937*. As the Church has declined, the writings of these early Scientists are becoming a vital part of the lifeline that is keeping pure Christian Science alive.

Basic Christian Science

One should read these notes in conjunction with other works on Christian Science, especially the works of Mary Baker Eddy, for they are based entirely upon her writings. These notes do not explore the whole of Christian Science, but they do go deeply into certain aspects of it which Mr. Young wanted to give the class.

To state simply the basic points covered in most classes:

1. Christian Science establishes God as the final cause of all things real. In the Christian Science textbook, *Science and Health with Key to the Scriptures*, by Mary Baker Eddy, God is defined as "The great I AM; the all-knowing all-seeing, all-acting, all-wise, all-loving, and eternal; Principle; Mind; Soul; Spirit; Life; Truth; Love; all substance; intelligence." Here we have an infinite Mind or divine Principle as the only cause or creator of the universe and man. This cause is not material or mental. It is spiritual, the one Mind filling all time and space.
2. Christian Science shows man and the universe to be the effect of the one Mind. Here Christian Science differentiates between the human mind and that spiritualized consciousness which understands God and man in His likeness. We read in *Science and Health*, "When man is spoken of as made in God's image, it is not sinful and sickly mortal man who is referred to, but the ideal man, reflecting God's likeness." When we understand the source or origin of man and the universe to be spiritual, we see that man and

ix

the universe are also spiritual, governed by the one Mind, all intelligent, wise, loving, just and good. Man embodies these Godlike qualities as his true selfhood. In reality, he is harmonious and perfect.

3. The divine logic of Christian Science shows that evil and matter, and all discord and adversity traced to them, are not from reality, but are the product of man's ignorance about reality. They are illusions resulting from false knowledge claiming that material laws and forces create and govern man. It is ignorance of God that causes all sickness, disease, lack, limitation, mental and emotional disturbance, discord, and adversity.

4. The allness of God and the unreality of evil can be proven through the unique form of prayer used in Christian Science known as *treatment*. This is far more than a prayer of supplication to God, or blind faith in Him, or resignation to adversity as the will of God. Treatment is a prayer of action. One takes the initiative and argues for the good, and against the evil or materialistic beliefs in consciousness. Through treatment one defends himself against evil thoughts and harmful hypnotic suggestions, while enlarging upon his understanding of God and man in His likeness.

These Class Notes are Mr. Young's teachings regarding this 'mental work' as it is called. A student of Christian Science first studies Christian Science, then he uses this understanding to pray intelligently or 'treat' his thinking in order to spiritualize it.

Healing Results of Prayer in Christian Science

Metaphysical work in Christian Science results in spiritual healing. Such healing work is not faith-healing, but healing based on a scientific understanding of reality. One studies Christian Science and learns to give a treatment in order to heal all forms of sickness and adversity.

Records of such healings are found in the last chapter of

Science and Health, called "Fruitage." The Christian Science periodicals dating from the 1890's carry thousands of verified testimonies of healings. Such healings are proof that the ideas set forth in Christian Science are true. A healing experience is evidence that one understands how to pray scientifically. This enlightenment is so powerful that it not only illumines consciousness, but also heals the body, regenerates the inner self, and blesses one's entire existence.

A New Language

As in all discoveries of such magnitude, Christian Science introduces a new language. Mrs. Eddy had to create special terms in order to communicate what she had discovered. This might be compared to the special language or terminology that one needs in order to understand music or computers. This new language is not hard to learn, and you should not be put off by it. The meanings of these words will unfold to you as you progress in a general study of Christian Science.

In these notes, Mr. Young has a number of references to Mrs. Eddy's writings — for example: *Science and Health* 242:12-16. This designates the book (*Science and Health*), the page (242), and the lines (12-16) to be read.

If you are new to Christian Science, these Class Notes are a strong introduction to it. Mr. Young was teaching very knowledgeable metaphysicians in 1937. Yet his ideas are most relevant to present day views. Those keeping pace with scientific progress know that world thought is passing through the illusion that matter is solid, that man is a biochemical machine, and that the universe is mechanistic. The final cause of all things lies in the dim unknown realm beyond the senses — a non-tangible dimension that can only be acknowledged subjectively and understood spiritually. Christian Science is the key to this kingdom within.

A. B.

NORMAL CLASS NOTES
OF 1937

NORMAL CLASS NOTES OF 1937

as taught by

Bicknell Young

Our first steps in pure metaphysics are made possible only through the simple process of affirming the truth and denying the error. That will always be an essential part of Christian Science education.

God is my Teacher. I am here incidentally. The only mind in Christian Science is the divine Mind; consequently that Mind revealing itself through right ideas, is the Mind of man. This man is to demonstrate Mind.

Human Mind

Whenever the human mind seems to be enlightened by right ideas, it is misleading to assume that mortal mind is entertaining right ideas. No such thing can occur. The term *mortal mind* designates the error, or belief, in a mind apart from God. That error is not capable of receiving enlightenment. It is capable only of extinction. The human mind does not receive ideas from the divine Mind. Ideas of the divine Mind are, on the contrary, the very presence of that Mind; and just in proportion to their presence, the beliefs of sin, sickness and death, which constitute the human mind, have no presence.

The divine Mind is Truth; human mind is error. It is contrary to Christian Science to attempt to mix Truth and error. Truth excludes error. If there is any point of contact (but there is no point of contact), it would be a point of expulsion.

1

We shall never arrive at the infallible demonstration of Science if we believe that the so-called human mind is becoming better. What is actually occurring step by step, is the demonstration of the one and only Mind, which will never become Mind because it is already and forever perfect Mind. This fact is not changed when, in the course of demonstration, human beliefs have the aspect of improved human beliefs. The consensus of opinion of human belief does not change the fact one bit. Whenever good appears in the thought or life of a human being, the belief is that there is something good in him. This is not so. Good is divine and not human.

Mind

Mind's demonstration of intelligence has never been reversed, interrupted, or impeded. Man's oneness with the intelligence and divine faculties of Mind, is forever demonstrated. A divine idea carries within itself the power to accomplish the divine purpose; and the responsibility of its unfoldment belongs to divine Principle, which cares for each detail of its progressive being. All the qualities of God, good, are expressed in man, His reflection; and no one quality or function is missing or inactive. There is a vast wealth of ideas hidden to material sense, but ceaselessly flowing from God and available to all. Mind expresses itself in continuous activity, in harmony, joy, and infinite unfoldment, in eternal self-renewal, in inexhaustible self-refreshment.

When Mrs. Eddy declared, "God is Mind," she brought about a religious revolution, for old religious thought had it — God *with* a mind. God *is* Mind, and we need to improve our understanding of this fact. Self-existent Mind is the source and substance of everything that exists. We must think God is Mind, not of God with a mind. Mind's characteristic is limitless intelligence.

Everything that Mind conceives is perfect and everlasting. God cannot conceive of anything contrary to His own selfhood. An idea is the only thing without restriction or limitation, for an infinite,

2

unlimited Mind cannot know of limited things. Every idea is unlimited, infinite. An idea cannot know anything about the limitation of space, time, or obstruction. Ideas are eternally alive, all intelligent, always active. Spirit is always active. Everything that is substance, is always active. Let ideas or facts be vital. Maintaining facts means that facts alone exist. Things, beliefs, and experiences contrary to facts, do not exist.

The entire objective consciousness is a dream. There is no subconsciousness. There are no planes of Mind; there is only one Mind. The only Science there is, is the Science of Mind. The true Science of all things is the Science of Life, or Being, and that is the Science of the divine Mind. Rely on Mind to do everything. God is our Mind, the only Mind there is. God fills all space. There is no material space; there is no limited space, such as four walls.

Mind is cause; therefore effect is idea. Cause is Mind; therefore effect is mental. Mind is the one and only cause, and cause must have an effect. We must hold in thought the fact that we reflect all intelligence. Mind is calm, serene, secure, supreme, always mindful of its own. You have the best mind on earth as effect, because you have the only Mind in heaven as cause.

Mind is the infinite intelligence of man, and everything that He knows is instantly available. Mind is never uncertain. One with Mind is absolute guidance. Truth is insistent, and quick to appear in the consciousness that is alert and receptive. *Mind is the infinite capacity to think*, and that is my mind. The greater our understanding of the one Mind, the greater our individual intelligence. Mind is infinite, and its ideas are forever progressive as expression. Divine thought always finds infinite expression. By substituting true knowledge for false belief, we demonstrate Truth. Man has one infinite Mind, and that Mind is my Mind and your Mind.

Spiritualizing thought is but getting away from limitation. A Christian Scientist stands as Mind. What he knows must govern the earth. We must recognize the power and dominion of Mind, which is all there is. Mind is the infinite capacity to think; it is con-

3

sciousness. Mind is the self-existence which we call God, and there is no other self-existence. Everything that exists is included in this Mind. Humanly speaking, all the Mind you have is in ideas. There is not a thought or idea in the universe that is not infinite. Keep this in mind. These ideas exist because they co-exist with the divine Mind.

There is no mystery in Godliness. Mystery and confusion come about through the human being's incapacity to understand infinity. We, as human beings, are all the time thinking of ourselves in a limited way; and now we come into Science, where there is no limitation; and here is where we must be wise, because we cannot consistently hold in thought two concepts of man — the real and the unreal, the unlimited and the limited. We cannot deny a thing and make it real at the same time.

Whether this life shall be one of dominion or subjection, is determined by the kind of thoughts we think. Thought is the only thing we have to deal with. All there is to anything is our consciousness of it. Do not think of yourself. What you know of God *is* yourself. Spiritual understanding comes more and more, and that is you. The dominion of man is simply the perfect law of God. Find out that you do not want anything, for that is dominion. It is not a matter of what others may be thinking. In the measure of our clearness, we are unassailable.

The only Mind there is, is right here; and we only need to claim it as ours to find how available God is to us. All of Mind is present with all of its infinite possibilities, and that is the law to this occasion. Claim your divine right to understand it *now*. It all belongs to you. Claim it and expect it. There is not a thing in the whole universe of Truth that is not yours right now. Individual man has at his disposal the infinity of ideas to apprehend forever. There is no limit to the possibility of unfoldment. There is a power always available to you that is greater than any human power and superior to any combination of circumstances. The thought which is in accord with God, is allied to omnipotence. Thought cannot be restricted in its power if it is correct.

4

Always insist upon having the wisdom that shows you what to do under any difficult circumstance. The thoughts that come to you everyday are bigger than the whole material universe, because they have always existed and are greater than space. All good is ours, and we attain it in the measure that we reflect it and *are* it.

> *Science and Health* 309:24-26; 505;7-12;
> 330:11-12; 6:5-6; 107:10-14
> *Miscellaneous Writings* 257:6-7

We must not only see what Mind is, but we must see by means of Mind itself. The whole thing resolves itself into this: that you cannot think *about* Mind, but you must think *as* Mind. That means that more and more, as Christian Science practice goes on, it is possible by means of the revelation of Christian Science to exercise divine power. It is not because you take a little of it and do something with it; it is because your thought is like it, is it, and acts as Mind itself. This Mind, infinite Mind, God, our Mind, is ever-present, always available law; and there is never a moment when it is inactive. The divine Mind doesn't have to learn anything, and this divine Mind is your heritage, and its understanding is spontaneous. Cultivate spontaneity. It is Godliness, purity and humility.

> *Science and Health* 260:13-18; 588:24-25;
> 591:16-20; 428:19-21
> *Pulpit and Press* 3:7-9

There is only one Mind, and that is my mind and your mind. No matter if you seem to be thinking error, that doesn't change the fact that the divine Mind is the only Mind that exists. A misapprehension of the truth doesn't change the truth, doesn't alter the fact that there is but one Mind. When Mrs. Eddy first began to establish this Cause, she used to say that God is the Mind of man more dogmatically than she did later. Not understanding that statement,

5

not perceiving that Principle is Mind, some of her students began to misinterpret it and taught students to say, "I am God." They perceived that there was but one Mind and that Mind was their mind, but they humanly wanted to claim divine power in such a way as to exercise omnipotence for their own selfish ends.

This error is as old as Bible history. Consequently Mrs. Eddy takes great pains to show the difference between God and man, and we must be clear about it. Many students, in making the distinction between God and man, have made a separation, and for years Christian Science has labored under that belief. They have made a separation, and at the same time they have claimed oneness. Mind and idea are one, and that one is Mind.

>*Science and Health* 302:19-24; 470:21-24;
>   477:20-25; 588:9-15
>*Miscellaneous Writings* 282:4-5
>*Miscellany* 117:19-20
>*Message of 1901* 5:14-16; 11:22-25
>*Retrospection and Introspection* pages 73-74
>*Rudimental Divine Science* 1:13 to 21 (next page)
>*Unity of Good* 7:8-21
>*Miscellaneous Writings* 361:28-31

Man is not God, but at one with God. Get their oneness, but also their distinctiveness and eternality. Each idea maintains its own individuality and identity forever. Every one of God's ideas is distinct and eternal. You would never confuse a rose with God, but it is always at one with God.

If you think you have two minds, you would be inconsistent; yet you are tempted to think: "Well here is my mind that is intelligent, and I know a lot, while I also know that God is Mind." Then you begin to reason in a wrong way. You have changed your terms but not your attitude, for when you say, "God is Mind," you are thinking of a distant God or a distant Mind. Now, right thinking is not the action of a distant Mind. If you want the Science of Being so that it will work invariably, always be in Mind, for your thinking must have the power, understanding, and law of that Mind; it must *be* that Mind.

Your affirmation in treatment must be from the standpoint of Mind declaring itself. It is not that we may know *about* that which is true, but that *we may know the Truth itself*, and that we may in some measure know the Truth, so that thought begins to be adjusted to divine intelligence, which is Truth. Christian Science requires of one who would demonstrate it *clearness of thought, intelligence, and ability to carry his thought to conclusions that are final.*

In order to do this, something more than intellectual thought is required. The pure logic of Christian Science requires the recognition of the divine nature, and the divine nature cannot be recognized by means of mere intellectuality. We may argue ourselves into a state where we can see the logic of Christian Science; but to demonstrate Christian Science, we have to do something more. Our own thought has to be Truth, unswerving Principle. It has to be Life. It is not enough that it should be what you think about these things; it must act directly as Life. Thought must be as it were God Himself thinking. That must be the thought, and that is more than intellectuality. Intellectuality is, generally speaking, useless; and though it seems to be a wonderful thing, it is insufficient. We are called upon to do much deeper thinking, far nobler, far more useful and more practical thinking, than the world has ever known. Therefore, our statements must not be made as though we are theorizing.

When we make our statements in a treatment, we must make them because they are true. It is not enough to declare the truth; we must *know* the Truth, and *know* that we know it. Truth is ever ready to reveal itself. The idea which reveals Mind *is* Mind. To see Truth is to see perfectly.

Ideas

Mind does not objectify itself. That would be separation. Ideas are Mind manifest. There is a distinction between manifest and manifestation. Everything exists eternally as an idea. Every idea is measureless. The substance of idea is indestructible; there is no disintegration. Lungs cannot be destroyed. Ideas cannot know or experience inaction, over-action, reaction, friction or fatigue. No idea is negligible. No idea can ever be destroyed. God, Mind, expresses His own infinite Being in ideas, and that means ideas are indestructible, imperishable, harmonious, substantial. An idea always maintains its own identity. All ideas are reciprocally blessing one another. They are never in conflict or trouble with each other. They can only bless each other because their origin is Mind, and Mind can only bless. Mind's ideas work together and cooperate. One idea can never be afflictive to another idea.

We sometimes say idea and at the same time think of the thing. The thing is not the idea. The object of study is enlightenment, and the object of enlightenment is idea. That is all you get. Study so that you get the idea as your own thought. Do not limit yourself. Get the idea which you perceive, and don't hold to a finite conception of a statement. Mind, being infinite, must comprise all that is true; therefore every right idea is essential to Mind. You can say to everything that exists in the universe: "That is an idea and is governed directly by Mind." Ideas are spiritually discerned and constitute true consciousness. Everything you are conscious of in a normal way, exists in a divine way, but not in matter.

There is a limited use to a human concept, but as divine idea it is unlimited; therefore, when you think, do not believe that you can be wearied or fatigued, that the brain has been exercised and you need a rest. Think with Mind and not with brain. Do not separate Mind from idea. Idea is Mind. Infinity is always harmonious, eternal and perfect, and cannot be humanly outlined. An infinite idea cannot swell, be enlarged, inflamed or impaired. There are not things; always see as idea. Ideas are tangible and real. The idea is more tangible and real than the material object, because the idea will go on. The idea is essential. The hand is an infinite hand. Mortal mind conceives of it materially as a useful part of the human body, but it is an immortal idea in the divine Mind. The embodiment of ideas is your real body. What we know is more tangible than our appearance, and eventually what we know will be our appearance. Every idea in the universe has the substance of Mind. It is real, tangible and eternal. All the Mind there is, is now.

Get rid of matter and declare the omnipotence of perfect Mind. "All that I have is thine;" and all that you have is never matter; it is always spiritual; and because it is always spiritual, it is always immediately available as the very presence of God that comes where you are thinking. There is no distance between Mind and idea, no space and no time. An idea is not the means by which divine Mind does something; it is the divine Mind in its manifestation. To know something of the natural presence of the divine consciousness, places us where we can instantly reflect the right idea which is the savior to the case. To know God as presence is the irresistible Christ to the case.

Do not try to treat as though you had power; treat as though you *are* power. All materiality is less than the truth you know. Never hesitate to handle life in matter. The right idea will always supplant the false belief. Resistance, time, weight, size, space, are all false concepts, and will disappear as the true idea is realized. They are nothing but limitation. Everything that God made exists as an infinite idea, and being infinite there can be no enlargement, swelling or disturbance to any of our faculties through the belief of inflammation or otherwise. An idea can never be confined, limited, or have a disease.

Being is Mind. Mind expresses itself as ideas. The divine idea is not a material object transformed by your imagination. That which exists divinely is idea. Before you could want anything, the idea would be present because that is the nature of idea. There is only one idea, and we all have it. Every idea is for each one. Each has it all. Everything exists as oneness, and cannot be humanly outlined. Do not think of God as being at a great distance. Mind and idea are not separated. The infinity of good belongs to each one, with nothing left out; no one can be deprived of anything. What is yours, is yours forever, and everything is yours.

Science and Health 327:29 (only); 494:19-20

Memory

There is quite a belief that one's memory can fail. That belief is based upon the claim that brains think; and when a person's brain reaches a certain age, it does not function as it should, and loss of memory results. You will have to understand that there is no thinking matter, and no inaction of mind can ever be impaired. Like reason, memory is human, but helpful. There are some things that memory should not be used for. As you get away from material sense and spiritualize your thought, memory will improve; man really does not have a memory, for that belief involves a forgetery. Man does not remember; he knows by reflection. Man knows as he has occasion to know. Nothing is ever lost from consciousness, the one Mind, for an instant; and as our mentality more and more approximates infinite consciousness, we shall be freed from the necessity of recording ideas. Memory is a word indicating the conscious nature of Mind in which truth is so vivid, constant and clear, that anything humanly essential may be recalled instantly; and everything that we may be entertaining that is unpleasant or humanly afflictive, may be properly and instantly obliterated.

Mr. Young told story about some friends calling on Mrs. Eddy one day. A servant told them she was in the back yard. They went around the house, and seeing that Mrs. Eddy seemed to be busy, they started away; but she called to them to come to her and then asked them if they knew what she was doing. They replied they didn't, and then she said, "I am going back in my memory just as far as I can remember and denying all error that ever seemed to happen to me." It is poor use of memory to review error. The real man has no memory of evil. Always live in the present; never mind the past or future. They are obviously unreal, and that which is unreal is nothing and nonexistent.

Everything is possible right now to man. The future holds no blessings that are not here and now. The Christian Scientist who is awake lives in the present moment, thoroughly enjoying it, for that is the only way to be equal to it. In a certain sense, there is no memory; there is only consciousness. Memory demonstrated is consciousness, the activity of Mind. In Science, you cannot forget anything. Get a clear understanding of the fact that you think with Mind and not with matter. As soon as Christian Science relieves you of the fear of a loss of memory, you learn there is nothing to forget. If you read something, you have it forever, for it is yours. Facts can never be forgotten or lost because they reside in Mind, and are instantly available to the Mind in which they have their being. There is one consciousness, and nothing is ever left out. Ideas are omnipresent like their divine source. The real man never remembers anything, because he knows all instantly. Consciousness just *is*, and that is the only memory — spontaneous knowing.

Attention is the human evidence of Mind, and should be directed to the enduring, the good and the true. Memory is a word the implies you can forget something. The fact is, it is impossible to forget anything. Life, harmonious and everlasting, is ever-present. Consciousness in Christian Science means much more than it does in philosophy. The unredeemed consciousness is not the child of God. Spiritual understanding is the Son of God. In knowing God, we reflect Him; and it is through the right knowing of God that the truth is reflected in our consciousness, and brought to bear on our human problems. As existence is consciousness, and the body is external-ized consciousness, the conditions of existence and of the body depend upon the state of consciousness. It is, therefore, necessary to change consciousness if we wish to change conditions. Christian Science will awaken human consciousness until it ceases to be human.

Question: What is Mind?
Answer: The infinite capacity to think.
Question: What is idea?
Answer: Expression.
Question: What is true consciousness?
Answer: God.

Chemicalization

Chemicalization is a term used by Mrs. Eddy in referring to the fermentation and transformation of mental chemistry which takes place when one thought changes or takes the place of another. It is helpful to recognize that there is a mental chemistry of disease and a moral chemistry of sin. In the case of sin, the chemicalization takes the form of a mental disturbance and aggravation, or change of condition itself, or a resistance to the healing, or a reaction against the healer or against the Truth itself. This sometimes appears when a strong moral thought of divine Principle is applied to an evil, sinful thought or habit which one is desirous of getting rid of. Never frighten your patients about chemicalization. Get them to rejoice.

The very fact that we exist involves the fact that there must be a cause for it. No one that ever lived is the cause of his own existence in any way. All the explanations of the human mind as to why we are here, are inadequate to explain our being here. The only thing that can and will explain it is Christian Science; and Christian Science does not explain it from a material basis, but from the basis of Truth, wherein is revealed the fact that the basis or foundation of all that exists is permanent, self-existent, without beginning or ending. In the light of reason, no explanation of cause would be satisfying to our thought unless it is on a permanent basis, without beginning or ending, and self-existent. Cause is self-existent entity, or consciousness. Self-existent consciousness is Mind, is one, and being one, is infinite. Infinity as defined in Christian Science is Principle, Love. Everything in the universe not only partakes of infinity, but is infinity expressed. There is nothing else to an effect but cause. The term *creator* is misleading. Creator in Christian Science means bringing to light, for creation has always existed. Get rid of the belief that things ever begin. There never was a time when everything did not exist. Of course, material things can change; but eternal things are forever self-existent, harmonious and perfect. Spirit is the creator of the universe. The only conclusion from that premise is that creation is spiritual, not material.

If God is entity, self-existent and eternal, and His creation is like Him, then nothing ever began or will ever end; everything has co-existence with God and in God. Don't take the halfway position in knowing this — that it will be true after a while. There is no theory about Christian Science. It is the Truth, and the Truth itself is all on the side of God, or the facts of being. If there is any such thing as theory, it is all on the side of that which is error, or false. The whole material sense of things is theory. So often one will see the absolute Truth as a beautiful theory, and he will say, "But of course, the facts are that we are here. We are all mortal; we have to eat and sleep and live materially; and we have to die someday," and other things along that line. Let us not take any part in that kind of error. Stand for Truth.

Of course, in your conversation with the average person, you cannot state the absolute facts of being; but you can always maintain them in your consciousness. You will have to talk to people in their own language, for they do not always understand the new tongue. Of course, in talking to them you are not trying to agree with them about the material sense of things; so do the best you can, and see that your own thought does not get down to mortal belief.

13

Nearly all physicists have a theory that there is an ultimate substance, but they are not willing to accept Mrs. Eddy's observation. They believe that there is an ultimate substance, and that it is the energy. They say that the substance we call matter is today returning to its original form; that in the disintegration of the present world, material forces are coming to light that have never been known, and they will be so available to us; that we will be able to do things by means of material science that are undreamed of because of the disintegration of matter; that all matter will revert to its original form, which is a theory.

All of the great physicists have arrived at conclusions that are epitomized in the following quotations of two noted material scientists. Professor Fiske of Harvard University says: "All the qualities of matter are what mind makes them and have no substance as such, apart from mind. Apart from consciousness there is no such thing as color, form, position, or hardness, and there is no such thing as matter." Charles Steinmetz in the *Atlantic Monthly* says: "It is not the province of physics to decide the nature of matter ultimately, its origin or end. That is the province of metaphysics, but it is the province of physics to deal with the phenomena as they are observed." Mrs. Eddy discerned by inspiration the things that these men are beginning to recognize by experimentation.

It seems necessary for us to know what the educated people in the world are thinking and doing. Material education must reach its zenith, must have its day, and all mortal mind beliefs give way to the teachings of Christian Science — that God, the first cause, is Spirit and that His universe is spiritual. When Mrs. Eddy says that the material body is the substratum of mortal mind, she states exactly what these men have been stating, because if it is true that matter by means of physical science is finally seen to be a theory; that it exists only in theory; that the material body is resolved into theory, then the body is the substratum of mortal mind according to material science.

If a theory is only a theory, it is nothing. If a theory has no foundation in Truth, then it is nothing; and we must conclude that if the material body exists wholly in theory, matter is a false claim, a limited sense of the divine idea. Creation is not going on in the ordinary sense. Man and the universe are infinite ideas. They co-exist with Mind, and being infinite, are forever unfolding the immeasurable perfection and grandeur of Mind. Human thought is interpreting spiritual creation and theorizing about it.

> I Chronicles 29: 10-14.
> David looking to God as sole creator.

Mr. Duncan Sinclair made a remark in Metaphysical College: "God is renewing His creation every moment." The whole sense of material creation is a myth. Creation is synonymous with man. All of the lesser ideas unfold through man. Revelation is the unfoldment of reality in human consciousness.

Creation

Because of its seeming inversion, diversion and restoration, we need to redeem our false inverted sense of creation.

In Romans Paul points out what a false sense of creation leads to.

We only sacrifice a material sense of things including the material body. We can only sacrifice sin, sickness and death, and evil beliefs.

Matter never becomes Mind. You can say there is no stone there. It is a counterfeit of the perfect idea. The material object is not the idea.

Substance

Spirit means substance. Spiritual means substantial. In this light, it is important that we become more sure each day of actual substance. Spirit signifies self-existent substance. Nothing is ever destroyed. There is not a single material object in the universe. All is spiritual. Principle, Mind, Soul, Life, are the cause of creation; and they are wholly mental, spiritual, tangible substance.

Science and Health 468:16-24

You cannot do a thing to Mind because it is substance. Harmony is then an essential quality of substance. The counterfact to discord is harmony. Harmony is the evidence of substance. Healing is proof of substance. Love is proof of substance. Mind, Principle, Soul and Spirit, are the substance of things hoped for by Christian Scientists. As one grows in understanding, he grows in substance; and what he gains, is incapable of discord and decay.

Creation is wholly Mind and is substance. There is no substance-matter, for matter is but a false concept of mortal mind, a mortal belief. Substance is the entity, or actual life, of a man.

Thought is perfect substance. Thought is indestructible. Anything you know of the Truth can never be destroyed. Thoughts which reveal God cannot be changed or dissipated. When you reach the point in your understanding of Christian Science that divine substance becomes real and tangible to you and your human body becomes subject to your understanding of substance, then you really have dominion.

You and I have the same substance, the same Mind, the same Soul, the same Spirit; and no one robs another of his substance. No one can lose his substance because another cannot have it. Both are satisfied. Both are complete. We have things by reflection. Substance is God, power, presence. Substance is immutable, immortal, harmonious, indestructible, unchanging perfection.

There is a belief that there is one substance to live and another to make a living. The divine Mind is the only substance, the substance that lives and the substance that makes the living. Anybody can get all the substance he wants by reflecting the divine Mind. Mind is substance — very useful to know.

The fact is, there is one infinite, eternal, indestructible substance, the one Mind. The idea of Mind is a tangible fact and not a thing. The idea of Mind has the substance of Mind in which it originates. Our substance is our being, and our being is eternal. You cannot find substance or man unless you look into Mind for them. Ideas constitute your Mind, and are its only substance. Ideas are the substance of Mind. Mind which is God cannot be outlined. God is infinite, immeasurable. God's law and action are substance.

Daily Protection

Know: The only man is divine, harmonious, invincible. His identity is a fixed fact in eternity, his substance is impervious to the belief of sin, sickness or death, and cannot be touched by the belief of danger or accident. The consciousness of the only man has no element of evil, destruction, condemnation, unhappiness, fear, anxiety, or limitation. There is nothing in the consciousness of the divine idea that can respond to the suggestion that such things even exist. They are unreal, and I know it. I am the divine Mind manifested, and that Mind cannot be handled. I and my Father are one. This day is God's day. The present moment and every moment of this day, are one of conscious contact with infinite good.

The law of infinite good, the law of divine Love, is the law of this day, and to all this day includes; and there is no other law. God's law is the law of Love, the law of wisdom, dominion and accomplishment, of clear perception, of perfect and accurate action, a law of perfect harmony to every event, circumstance, incident, and detail of this day. It is the law that dissipates the belief of passing time, and destroys the claim of haste, because Mind rests in action. The law of harmony and love is the law to everything that I shall think, say, or do, that shall occur with the radius of my thought or experience this day or any day forever.

There is no mental malpractice and no mental malpractitioner. There never was a first one. The belief of mental malpractice is a mindless and lawless falsehood, an impossible belief without a believer. As a belief, it is annulled by the activity of the Christ in Christian Science practice. The belief of mental malpractice has no mind and no capacity to think. It cannot act or operate in belief or at all; and my understanding of Christian Science, which is God with us, annuls the belief of malpractice in regard to this day completely and absolutely.

Love

First, last and always, the great need is Love. Lack of love is the only trouble with the world today. Love alone will heal the distrust, jealousy, fear, and ignorance of the race; and in doing this, it will heal its lack and disease. Love is Life, and its seeming absence is death. Any human being might be justified in not liking another person, but he should still love him. There would be something the matter with you if you liked them all.

You cannot like the unpleasant and objectionable things and call that love. You can love the real man, but if a human being seems to express nothing but evil, you cannot like him, and you cannot say that he is the son of God. The real man is the son of God; and that is all that is true about him. Anything else is an illusion, and a misrepresentation. Love is so powerful that when the individual demonstrates it to the extent that it is the only Mind he has, it will do something to everything he comes in contact with. If it arouses hate, he can say he is sorry, but it has nothing to do with him.

Jesus was never more loving than when he scourged the money changers out of the temple, but it seemed a whip to them. Love will do things to that which is untrue and wicked, that the untrue and wicked will feel. It is important to see that divine Love is Principle.

Love is unfailing, never changing, always active and available; in fact, it is the basis of all creation. The statement, "God is

18

Love," is the most metaphysical in the Bible. Human love is full of fear and doubt; however, it is not to be destroyed, but redeemed. We do not lose human affection in Christian Science; we lift it up. Don't stifle human affection, but let it be more and more like God.

Elevate your thought of man and love more. You not only have to recognize divine Love, you have to *be* divine Love. Divine Love is not a distant power that meets human needs. Divine Love will do nothing for a man until he takes it into his consciousness. [Told of a man who went to see a practitioner and he said to him, "Christian Science says, 'Divine Love meets every human need!' why haven't I been healed?" The practitioner said to him, "Where is your divine Love?"]

Mrs. Eddy always worked from the standpoint that disease could not stand where Love is. We need not only to believe in Love, but to live in Love, to be Love, and to know that there is no other being than Love. Love is the acme of all things; and Love is the divine Principle of all being, the Mind that is God, and the Life that is man. Love is the only essential Principle of the universe, and you cannot go beyond Principle. [Told of Mrs. Eddy simply surrounding a tree with love in the middle of winter while the ground was covered with snow, and bringing blossoms out on it just as if it were the middle of spring. Also told of a man in England who had a garden and one year a heavy frost came up; his wife said she would handle it. The man had one rose bush he valued very much, so he said he would throw a little straw over the bush. It was the only thing in the garden that died.]

False Beliefs about God

1. God is like a human being. This is an anthropomorphic error. The belief has four fallacies:

    a. God is partial, and has His favorite sons. He does no such thing. Man is the son of God individually and collectively. "Love is impartial and universal in its adaptation and bestowals." (*Science and Health* 13:2)

      b. God is changeable. This idea has darkened all history. James 1:17

      c. God answers prayer by special intervention. This has many evil results and ends in priesthood.

      d. God suspends His law and at times it does not act. Many believe that God suspended His law for Jesus.

2. God is not entirely good. If God is not entirely good, He knows both good and evil. God does not know evil, or of evil.

3. God acts through curse, penalty or punishment. God employs or sends evil. Evil is self-punished. Principle is the rod of iron to error. Evil will always break itself to pieces against Principle, the rod of iron.

4. God is finite or limited.

5. God is absent or somewhere unexpressed. Man is separated from God. Man does not completely reflect God. There is no lack of good anywhere.

6. Jesus is God. He never said he was.

7. God consists of three persons. This error became established about the third century.
Christian Science vs Pantheism 9:3-4

8. Material man is included in God. That God is in every material thing. This is pantheism. God is in all, but not in matter. God does not use matter in any way to shine through.

Science and Health 302: 19-24;
    477:20-25 (Identity); 470:21-24; 588: 9-15

Treatment

No Christian Science practitioner has ever had a real disease to cope with. There never has been and never will be such a thing as a disease in the whole universe of Truth. When a patient comes for treatment and says he is suffering from tuberculosis or any other claim, the practitioner knows that the only thing that has to be destroyed is what the patient thinks about the suggestion of the disease.

When the belief in disease is destroyed, nothing remains to express the disease. Analyze the false beliefs, then offset them with correct statements of the Truth.

Science and Health 233:28-29

The counterfact is the Christ idea to the case. "Ye shall know the Truth, [the counterfact] and the truth shall make you free."

Science and Health 400:18-22; 411:27-1;
    415:24-26; 412:4-9

It is a strange thing how some Christian Scientists expect to succeed when they declare the Truth one minute and voice error the next. Every now and then you hear someone complain that error does not at once yield to his declaration of Truth. The fact is that while the declaration of Truth is a step in the right direction, it is not always sufficient to overcome evil. One's thoughts, words, and deeds, must be in harmony with his declarations. The mere declaration of the letter is not enough. The recital of correct arguments without spiritual perception, is not Christian Science treatment.

21

To affirm the Truth mentally is only the beginning of one's work. We must also affirm the Truth practically, letting our lives bear witness to the good. If evil is nothing in theory, it should be nothing in practice. It should be treated as nothing in both cases.

When a treatment is given, the student brings to bear upon some specific lie all the knowledge of Truth he has acquired since he first began to study Christian Science. A treatment is not a practitioner thinking about a patient. A treatment is Truth handling error. Christian Science does not make error unreal; it *proves* error unreal. Christian Science does not create health; it *reveals* health. The spiritual idea used for restoration, is the counterfact. The moment the counterfact is realized, the healing takes place.

Nothing is more important to us than that we should be thoroughly practical. Christian Science treatment would be robbed of its purpose and intention if the spiritual harmony is not to be humanly evident. It is absolutely necessary for one to know that the treatment which declares a divine fact operates as divine law, and that it enforces the divine law in human experience. The best way to do this is to know the unity of divine Mind and idea.

"The Lord said to my Lord, Sit thou at my right hand, till I make thine enemies thy footstool." (Mark 12:36) Now, that simply means that God, the omnipotent, infinite power that is God, says to my understanding: "When you get the right idea, the counterfact, stick to it and maintain it until the end of error." Everything that is true, sits at the right hand of God, for Truth is one with God and has the power of God in it. Every thought that comes to you in the realm of absolute truth, sits at the right hand of God and gives you divine authority and dominion to successfully and scientifically and unerringly annul and destroy the claims of false mortal belief.

You should never take the attitude of some people who say the work is done, when there is no material evidence of its being done at all. That will never do — never. We have to demonstrate the healing, and not merely assume that it has been accomplished when the patient still manifests the claim. Keep at it until there is no evidence of a physical claim, until the disease is removed completely. Stick to the work until the false evidence vanishes through your treatment.

When the patient begins to improve, you must not let down in your work. This is just the time to be awake and destroy the claim, root and branch. Diligently and faithfully keep treating until there isn't a trace of it left. It is not wisdom, nor is it strictly true, to say that the demonstration is made when the final evidence is not as it should be. This is sometimes said, but it is not a good thing to say. It gives a wrong impression, and is not strictly true, even on a basis of human honesty. While it is true that wonderful benefits are experienced by patients who do not recover, let us not lose sight of the fact that they should recover.

No matter what the testimony of the senses, you must stand. One cannot assume that he has demonstrated Science until the testimony of the senses changes favorably. Even then we cannot rest upon the favorable change, but upon the divine Principle and rule by which the change was brought about. In stating spiritual facts and realizing them, keep your feet on the ground. Be sane and practical; and when you declare the spiritual nature of man, make it so practical that the law of your statement is immediately available to the man who thinks he is still material and who appears to be material. Let spiritual Truth become a law to the person right where he seems to be in belief. Watch out for mere exaltation, for exaltation is certainly not Science.

It is necessary for us as Christian Scientists to establish the divine consciousness as the natural, primal Principle of all the incidents of life, and let that divine consciousness or Principle operate through its omnipresence in everything we do humanly.

It is essential that treatment declare that the law of divine Mind to the divine idea, is also a law to every belief about that idea, and because of your treatment, is *law;* the belief has no continuity.

Science and Health 282:26

Trust in what God knows. The great and all-important thing in the work of a Christian Scientist is to know, and his knowledge is something entirely apart from the realm of mere belief. Therefore you can readily see how we can heal the sick while we still go around with (what appears to be) a material body and a limited sense of life. We go about in a limited way among people (apparently) and do a lot of things that are wholly in the realm of belief; and yet when a patient comes for help, we reject all that false environment and life, and live in the realm of absolute Mind. Jesus walked the earth like other men (apparently), had a material body, and did material things (apparently); but the moment someone came to him for help, notwithstanding that he himself (apparently) manifested a belief of material existence, which is error, his thought was so clear and strong that he healed them instantly and raised the dead.

When you handle error as a mere secondary expression of the primal error, mortal mind, you are handling it scientifically. When you permit your thought to be so handled that you believe that you must actually contend with some difficulty, and that the difficulty has some substance, power, law or operation, you are not working correctly. Whatever the error is, its only substance is supposition, whether the error be lack, pain, malice, opposition, or what not. It has no substance other than supposition, and the supposition has no supposer. The belief has no believer, for the believer is a belief. The counterfact must be absolutely spiritual. Mental practice should always be affirmative.

Science and Health 207:27-4; 418:20-25

Even your denials must be made from an affirmative basis. In treatment start from Principle, and do not limit yourself. Mental practice is a process more or less, and the Truth must be declared relative to the supposition.

The process consists of three parts:

1. Resolving things into thoughts or beliefs.
2. Seeing these beliefs as inversions of reality.
3. Then realizing the absolute Truth.

Know the perfection of the spiritual idea in order to restore the normal condition. Treatment is the process leading to realization which heals. If realization is made without process, and is immediate, so much the better; but the practitioner to be depended upon, is the one who can give a clear treatment, who is always absolute. You must have clear affirmation, and must get clear realization.

Even your denials must have the strength of strong affirmation. The Christ, the power of God, is actually saving mankind. Your conviction and faith in your understanding makes your treatment invincible. The patient is always helped by the practitioner's faith in his own ability to demonstrate Christian Science.

In giving a treatment, see that it is well defined, having purpose. Make your treatments forceful, scientific, and exact. We do not argue to resist error, but to know its nothingness. Be as big and as free in your treatment as you can possibly be. Be as much like God as possible. The more nearly you think as God thinks, the better your treatment will be. When you are working on a case, do not think too much about results, for when you are not thinking about results, you get better results. Let consciousness be redeemed, and do not even think about results. Be conscious of divine facts as if you *are* the facts, and Principle will take care of its own results.

Never let "how long" enter the case. Perfection is the ever-present now. It is essential to know that everything that needs to be in a treatment will be in it. If you go into details, handle it thoroughly. Bring the treatment down into the realm of human need so that the divine facts become a law to the human belief or seeming condition. Divine law is operating in human affairs, and don't doubt it. Divine law is humanly demonstrable.

While it is true that all treatments are impersonal, and the more impersonal the better, still you cannot just send a treatment into the air. That kind of treatment isn't any good at all. If your treatment is not doing something specifically, it is not doing anything at all as far as the patient is concerned. Never try to picture or imagine a healing, for much harm can come from this error. There is no error anywhere. The concept of matter is wholly false and impossible. We do not have to deal with matter at any time.

As long as the belief seems to be in matter you are not making it nothing. Always get it to be nothing, and never leave disease in matter or in belief. In every treatment, God must be understood to be all power, all presence, all Mind, substance, Principle, intelligence, action, and the perfect law of His own creation.

To heal the human body, one needs to know the truth about it; and the truth about it is that identity is not human, but divine. This is also true about everything that seems to constitute the human body. The object of Christian Science is to prove the power of God in human affairs. Christian Science is the Science of whatever you are doing. As existence is consciousness, and the body is eternalized consciousness, the condition of existence and of the body depends upon the state of consciousness. It is necessary therefore to change consciousness in order to have changed conditions.

Prayer and Supplication

Science and Health 1:11-14; 2:28-30; 13:5-19
Pulpit and Press 22:5-8
Miscellaneous Writings 127:7-16; 220:4-15
No and Yes 39:2-4

Mental practice in a personal manner, is not a personal treatment. You seem to be addressing a person. This is a very crude way, but permitted. It is not a very good way to work; but you sometimes seem to get results in this way. It is well to be cognizant of this way of working and how to do it if necessary.

This is just as though you were addressing the thought of the person. The danger of this system is that if you use error instead of Truth in your argument, you would be using hypnotism.

Science and Health 376: 18-26; 377:1-3; 417:20-21

If you have to speak, speak to the error.

Mark 4:39: "And he arose, and rebuked the wind, and said unto the sea, Peace be still." Jesus was addressing the error.
Luke 4:8: "And Jesus answered and said unto him, Get thee behind me, Satan."
Luke 4: 19: "And he stood over her, and rebuked the fever; and it left her: and immediately she arose. . ." Jesus rebuked the error, and not the woman. Error claims to be mental, and it seems sometimes if we talk to it, it goes away.

Science and Health 395:6-10
Retrospection and Introspection 61:13-20
No and Yes 13:1-3

Always talk to error and not to the sick person. To treat a case means to handle the claims of error in the case and not the person.

No and Yes 23:18-22
Science and Health 377:20-25

There is always a leading error in the case. You are really a mental analyst, and can get the counterfact as the patient states his case to you as he goes along. You should expect to heal the case while it is being stated to you.

Mental Practice in an Impersonal Manner

Miscellaneous Writings 359:4-7; 350:26-30
Science and Health 11:21-22; 4:3-5; 411:3-12;
    376:18-26; 12:2-15;
    366:30-9; 454:31-2; 15:9-13

The less of personal sense in your work, the better. Your treatment should always be absolutely and not personally worded. This is the correct way for a well taught Scientist to work. Truth reaches and deals with every individual case.

Science and Health 1:1-9; 14:12-16; 16:20-23;
    233:17-22; 312:5-7;
    450:19-26; 460:14-18
Rudimental Divine Science 13:18-22
Message to The Mother Church of 1901 20:8-9

Knowing

The ultimate method of practice or treatment:

Miscellaneous Writings 116:20-24; 352:23-27;
    220:21-2; 46:11-25
Science and Health 447:27-29; 454:31-2; 566:30-8

The more of the Gabriel method, the better, without argument. In addressing the patient audibly or inaudibly, know the Truth. In the absence of immediate realization, correct affirmation and denial is the way of demonstration.

Establish the facts about God and man in your consciousness, and maintain them throughout your treatment. The object of the argument is to arrive at some measure of realization. The *modus operandi* will differ according to the Scientist and his progress.

Disease in any form is never anything but a belief. Take cognizance of it as a belief, but only as a belief. You do not have to change matter, just change the belief. Resolving error into thought is only one step. Get it into thought and finish it up. Make it nothing.

The definition of error is *illusion*. The thing you are treating is in the realm of belief and has no more substance than one's belief permits. When you reach the point in your treatment where error is nothing, your treatment is successful.

Your treatment must give a thorough defense in the letter. There must be correct statement in the letter, otherwise the results will be very uncertain. Be thorough in your work and leave no loophole in your treatment. Clear scientific thinking gives the ability to unravel a claim to its utter nothingness.

When you give a treatment, do not attempt to apply Science, but get to the point where your thought *is* Science. The real treatment is Science, Mind, immediate realization without conscious effort. All real treatment is the naturalness of God's presence, illustrating the unlabored motion of the divine energy in healing the sick

Science and Health 445:20

Treatment is the idea or Word of God made active, operative, demonstrable in human experience. The false evidence of the claim is repudiated by your understanding of the allness of God and the perfection of man. Understanding is never afraid. When the thought becomes spiritual, triumphant, error cannot stand.

Do not belittle your understanding. Have great confidence in your understanding of Truth. Confidence and understanding are omnipotent and invincible. Do not treat as though you had power, treat as though you *are* power. Treat as though it is power being exercised.

You can heal one disease as readily as another. The best treatment in Christian Science is when the pure sense of divine being is so completely affirmed, when consciousness is so flooded with spiritual light without argument, that it is adequate as a realization of the perfection of man. That is the sum of Christian Science, and far better than any system or *modus operandi*; but we have to be prepared for anything in the practice; therefore we must be able to argue.

The action of Mind is direct action. There is no matter and no material personality to be healed. All that confronts us is mortal mind, so deny mortal mind. Make your analysis impersonal, and do not think of the patient.

You must be happy when doing your work. Maintain joy throughout your work and in your lives. A real treatment is not an argument of contention, but of dominion. What you are thinking is the dominating influence which dissipates the error.

Let your treatment know enough to know it is good. A good rule for treatment is to start with clear, affirmative statements, then an adequate denial, then again affirm the truth about God and man, and leave the case.

Be specific and accurate. Look out for the tendency to say, "God will take care of it. It will work out all right," and then idly wait for something to happen. That is faith cure, and no good could come out of that slipshod way of handling a case.

What is generally called "trusting God" is mere indolence, old theology; and there is no security in that kind of trust in God. Treatment must have dominion, power, and the presence of God, and nothing less than that, because it is your treatment. Don't think of yourself as a younger student; the first shall be the last.

Understanding is not measured by time. Don't get a false sense of humility that is as weak as water. Get your unity with God; unity without personal pride. Exalt your Science and forget yourself. You cannot heal without humility. "I and my Father are one," is the most perfect self-denial ever voiced. This great humility enabled Jesus to say, "Be of good cheer, I have overcome the world." This great humility was the secret of his great dominion. In fact, it takes great dominion to be humble.

Always handle the claim that another treatment is necessary. We should not expect to have to treat the patient tomorrow. That mental reservation will perpetuate the claim, and is nothing but animal magnetism. A real treatment is perfection operating as divine presence and law, not only declaring the Truth, but demonstrating it. Your practice and treatment must be systematic, logical, and at the same time inspired, not limited or restrained.

You cannot tabulate diseases and their so-called causes — that is, assume that a certain disease is due to a certain cause. You do not always find the mental cause. If it doesn't come to you clearly that there is something mentally wrong with the patient, don't assume it; handle the patient from the standpoint of God.

Rheumatism

God is Mind, Spirit, Life; the source, substance and condition of all being; the Soul and Life of man. The only cause, the only Father-Mother of the universe, is the one ever-existent entity, and man is one with and inseparable from God as His expression of perfection and completeness. Man is the perfection of the divine being expressed. His identity is forever maintained in peace, completeness, harmony, and love. The divine man, as God's own idea, is without beginning of years or end of days.

Man is not subject to sin, sickness, age or death. He is co-existent with God, the divine Principle, in which he has his being. There is no rheumatism; there is no cause for rheumatism, no law under which it can operate, and no substance in which it can appear or control.

Mind is the only creator, and made all that is made. Man is spiritual, perfect and eternal. There is no obstruction of harmonious action. There is no poisonous substance in blood. Blood is not a fluid; it is thought, a divine idea, uncontaminated, pure; and its circulation is the movement of omni-action, without any obstruction or anything that can interfere with its harmony and perfect activity.

The law of the divine idea is the law of perfection, joy, harmony, health and continuity. There is no other law. This treatment establishes the fact that there can be no continuity to the false belief, and as a false belief it is destroyed by this treatment, and there is nothing left to it in belief or at all. There is no rheumatism. That is the name of a nameless lie, a name that means nothing, for there is no disease of any kind, visible or invisible. In infinity, there is no law but the law of Love; and under the law, which is made operative through this treatment, the belief of rheumatism cannot exist, or be perpetuated, or have any being, action or evidence.

Substance is Spirit and all, and in Spirit there is no disease. There is no matter in which it could claim to have manifestation, for matter is a false belief without entity, and cannot embrace or express disease. The law of being is perfection. Being itself is perfection, and there is no other law to consciousness or to man. There is no rheumatism. It is impossible because God is all, and everything that exists expresses God.

In these modern times, rheumatism is frequently considered a disease of the brain; and knowing that, I would handle that. Some claim that it is poison from the teeth, and that it affects the blood. Others say that it is acidity, and still others that it is nerves. If your patient is a Christian Scientist, handle malpractice. Know that there is no law of rebound when you are treating a patient, and you think you begin to feel as he does.

Man includes ideas because the universe consists of ideas and nothing else. It does not consist of persons with ideas; the ideas are man. Christian Science teaches that Mind expresses itself in ideas, and nothing else could express Mind.

Man is the embodiment of right ideas. These ideas never mingle with matter, and so are forever free from all its conditions. For example, wisdom is never affected by blood circulation, nor justice by the action of the heart; goodness cannot have a fever; mercy cannot ache or feel a pain; kindness cannot be operated upon; nor can gratitude meet with an accident.

Business

Very often the trouble in business arises from the fact that the human being doesn't know his business. Know your business in a human way. Some people think Christian Science can do things like magic, but it cannot do anything to a man's business until the man himself is changed. The success is in man before it is in his business.

Psalm 1:1-3

Business demonstrations come along the natural lines of human experience, and you must use good common sense. It is not all Elijah going up in a chariot, but much of it is the cruse of oil that shall never fail. If you are getting along all right today, there is no reason to believe that God will neglect you next week.

The first thing to do, is to see that man is a state of infinite possession. All opportunity is his. Heaven is his; the infinity of good belongs to him. Man exists at the standpoint of opportunity, not once, twice, nor alone in human experience, but forever; and man is capable of seeing it. Opportunity is mental, not material; and no condition, position or circumstance can take it away. The opportunity to cast out the false and give place to the true, is ever-present to all mankind equally; and no law of heredity, education, environment, or habit, can shut out any man from the opportunity to acquaint himself with God and be at peace.

In business, we have to use what mortal mind calls matter, and we have to calculate with what mortal mind calls money. The only thing you get for nothing is Spirit, and of course that is all we need. If we had all the Spirit we could have for nothing, we would have all the money we want, to buy all the (apparent) matter we need.

One says, "Oh, divine Love will provide everything," just

as if divine Love were something very wonderful, way off some place, showering things on a human race. The fact is, divine Love has nothing to do with man until he takes it into his consciousness. The very nature of Love is such that it never heard of withholding; consequently, wherever Love is, there cannot be anything less than infinite abundance.

The average person coming into Christian Science, when he learns that God is Love, thinks he is liable to become soft as dough, and that is just what mortal mind would like! The state of thought is very gullible; and such a person will find that he has become weak, instead of strong. For that reason, watch and pray that you be more intelligent in business than you were before, for one of the phases of mortal mind is, that it sees you are a little less sharp than you were before, and it takes advantage of it. Divine intelligence makes you many times sharper than the non-Scientist.

Business exists wholly in Mind as God's idea. Man's business, my business, the only business there is, is in its place forever; and it is forever active. It has its foundation in divine Principle. Its law is divine law. It is self-sustained and perpetuated by the law of infinite harmony. It belongs to man. It is his legitimate heritage from God, and is forever unfolding; and there is nothing the matter with it now or forever.

No claim of lack or mental suggestion on the part of any so-called human being, nothing mortal mind can say, can darken this heritage. The false claim of lack or fear, is animal magnetism, without being, organization, existence, or law; without place, space, or occupancy. Any sense of fear has no effect on this business or any relation to it.

This business is the manifestation of wisdom, and this wisdom is the manifestation of God, and this natural manifestation is man. Man does not know how to lack wisdom, ability or light. This wisdom is present now, and through this treatment it is made available. There is no mortal influence, opinion, or suggestion, that can touch this business in any manner known or unknown.

What we have to learn to do, is to dignify the thing we are doing. You have got to bless your business, redeem it, save it, and recognize its impulsion as divine. Things we are doing outwardly are beautiful and grand, if the basis and incentive are in Principle. If we are moved by divine power and Love, our actions are blest and sustained by that law. Make Principle more practical in actual life.

Thinking is a big thing. Don't make it little. Thinking is your business. Think in a big way; it is much easier than thinking in a little way. The bigger thinking is, the better it operates in a specific instance. Don't be afraid to see it operate in a universal way.

Science and Health 84:14-18; 258:25-25; 514:6-9

When true enlightenment comes, man does business with more breadth and capacity. He knows that his business is not governed by circumstance; it is governed by God. Put your understanding at the head of affairs. Keep your dominion, and you will be called upon to do things in a larger way.

Business is primarily something that is active, and business is something that could have no being at all if it were not all in God. In selling anything, it must bless the buyer or there should be no buyer. Principle requires honesty in seemingly little things.

Truth is Principle, because it is always right. Your primary business is so absolutely fixed in God that nothing can ever touch it; and if the secondary thing looks bad, look away from it, so that you are not mesmerized by it. The real man's supply is secure, eternal, enduring, untouched by fluctuations, inaccessible to jealousy, interruptions, injury, or dishonesty.

Man has been created solely for the realization and expression of harmony. Everything that blesses man is God's will. Success is that which is given to you infinitely; and you can never fail to have it, and the abundant evidence of all its infinite blessings.

People say they possess all things, but we know it is quite different. Never make a statement in Christian Science that does not come from conviction and understanding. Avoid superficial statements.

The Christian Scientist maintains Truth in his consciousness until it becomes his consciousness; and as it becomes more pure and serene, more surely can it be demonstrated. Sometimes he goes on drifting with mortal mind; but there comes a time of reckoning; and the hard time that he has, is the greatest blessing that could ever happen to him. It wakes him up. An easy time never made a good Christian Scientist.

All business exists in the divine order. It is all God's business. God's business is the ceaseless activity of infinite ideas, always harmonious, successful beyond expression, and absolutely infallible. God's business is already established; its laws are mutually beneficial, blessing one and all. God's business is never intermittent and never interfered with. It exists by virtue of ceaseless law. Business is in heaven — all of it. Business must be as legitimate as healing, if it is carried on in the right way. Demonstrate business by Principle. No matter how bad things look, hold on. That anything is lacking, is only the denial of oneness; and all of it is as unreal as a ghost. When you get to the end of your rope, tie a knot and hold on.

Man was never in trouble. You must handle details from the standpoint of God. Principle, God, enforces His law by virtue of His own presence and power; and that means that you do not have to make the divine Mind do something. Its presence is quite sufficient; and in proportion that you understand this presence, it will take care of the situation, no matter what it is.

There is constant temptation to a business man or woman to do something that is a little bit undesirable or questionable from the standpoint of divine Principle. You will be importuned to take part in, invest in, or associate with, or in some manner involve yourself in, a business where, if you look deeply, you will find nothing but dishonesty. *The short cuts to wealth will be invariably dishonest.* It is a constant temptation to get rich quick, and it is absolutely essential that the people who come under that claim should break away from it. You cannot enter the practice of Christian Science and heal the sick and raise the dead, if you are still tempted by that claim, because that sort of thing does not mean you shall love your neighbor as yourself, but that you shall do him in.

There are questionable business methods, and there are many of them. You will be tempted to enter some form of business procedure that is not straight. Your associates will say, "It is all right; everybody does it," which is a very good reason for you not to do it. The moment you refuse, you have a kind of distinction. There is plenty of legitimate business, and a Christian Scientist has nothing to do with any other kind. Business is not just making money, though business must pay; but the main object is not to make money. Those organizations and individuals that operate only for personal gain cannot prosper.

The object of business in its highest sense, humanly speaking, is to serve mankind, through production, or supply, taking care of human needs; but in a still higher sense, it is knowing what God is, and knowing God aright. If you appear to have a business that is apart from God, immediately know that your business is one with God, because you are thinking of your business, and your thinking is all there is to your business so far as you are concerned. All the business you have, is your consciousness of business. You may be sure that in your business, as in everything else, if you think rightly, there will be revealed to you unmistakably the successive and progressive steps you are to take.

If you need combinations, they are already made in divine Mind. If you need capital, it is there without measure. The best capital is faith in one's self, not as a mortal, but as an intelligent expression of Principle; and if your business is not paying, get it where it ought to be in thought, and it will pay an hundred-fold.

Know that you are expressing divine Principle and that it knows no limitation; and because you are one with it, it is giving you all things to enjoy. Love has already provided everything. Love not only meets every human need, but anticipates it; long before a human need can be felt, Love has already provided for it; you only need to love in order to have all things in abundance and find peace forever. It is not fundamentally money that is needed, but Love, confidence and intelligence.

In Christian Science, the supply is always mental, always ideas. The only poverty there is, is lack of knowledge of God. God's presence is at hand to supply every need, and He has provided for us an infinite wealth of spirituality, and this true income is sure, timely, and adequate.

As God's spiritual reflection, man has boundless opportunities, infinite capabilities, ceaseless occupation. His capital is Mind, unlimited and available at all times, in all places, and under all circumstances. Man possesses all that he requires to conduct his business harmoniously and successfully. Since every idea was created as a part of God's all-inclusive plan, there is not an idle, useless or superfluous idea in the universe. Each idea was created to fill its place and to do its allotted work. Its position is the place it occupies in the divine Mind, from which it can never be displaced, misplaced, or replaced. Divine Mind governs, maintains, supports, and supplies His spiritual universe, including man.

Error is bankrupt. Its currency is counterfeit; it has no credit, no resources, no supply, no existence. Man, reflecting God, possesses a supply of countless ideas. There is a right source of infinite good to which every man and woman may apply with success for his supply, for his wisdom, strength and sustenance.

As we turn from our outward barrenness and seek to lay off spiritual penury, as we cease from beholding the shortcomings of others and begin correcting our own, as our whole purpose is dedicated to service and we strive to be rich in giving, we let go of poverty — of the only hold that poverty has on us; and we are then able to grasp the only true substance.

Mortal limitations of time and circumstance are bound to disappear as Truth is understood, since Principle is the same yesterday, today, and forever, and remains unaffected by these apparent conditions, though they shake the human belief of the universe from end to end.

If all reality exists in the divine Mind, and lack never began there and does not exist in real consciousness; it is obvious that that which never had a beginning does not have to finish; but the right time is right now in which to get rid of our belief in lack or any other form of error or limitation, and gain the true sense of Mind as substance.

The Christian Scientist knows that in giving he is not separating himself from good, but rather reflecting the infinite sufficiency of his Father-Mother God, and that he is not consuming substance, but utilizing the infinite, unlimited resources of the infinite Mind.

The Christian Scientist who perceives this true substance, can give fearlessly to his church or to his business, having learned the difference between giving and giving away, using and using up.

There is no material law of supply and demand in Mind; there is nothing but supply. There is no requirement. God is limitless, eternal, ever-present Mind or intelligence, the one Life made manifest in all His creation. Mind cannot accumulate, absorb, or deplete. Truth cannot accumulate; it is ever-present, eternal, indestructible, knowing neither beginning or end, increase or decrease. It is all.

The supply is as unlimited as the Supreme Giver Himself. There is an unlimited supply of divine ideas, and the activity of any idea can never be impaired, depleted, or exhausted. Nothing exists that can stop the flow of substance from the divine Mind and its continuous impartations, for an infinite source has no need of accumulations.

True supply is the flow of infinite good into human consciousness, a continuous unfolding in the everlasting *now*. Man is a constant manifestation of intelligence and unending life. He has wisdom, strength and ability to accomplish his divine purpose of expressing infinite good.

Science and Health 215:11-14

When we realize the grandeur, beauty, harmony and perfection of the real man in Christian Science, we see that no material condition or circumstance can add to, or take away from, his true substance. That which constitutes infinity never comes or goes. Nothing can be added to it or taken away from it. It is unchanging completeness. The supply requisite to meet any demand, is now and here in Mind; and it is yours for the accepting at any time. Mind is the presence and substance of every idea. The moment Scientists break the claim of wanting something, they will find peace.

Infinite Mind has no hidden resources; they are ever-present and available. Mind is always revealing its blessings to its own creations. You should never say, "God gave me so and so" — you always had it. There is no demand; it is all here. Man does not need to ask for anything. He has everything; and Christian Science reveals it absolutely, and is the only power in the universe that knows how to uncover good and bring it to pass.

Fear

In handling this claim, remember that mortal mind is the basic error. (*Science and Health* 405:1) The outstanding thing about fear is its foolishness. Fear is a part of every claim. Fear, when it becomes acute, can easily become hate and malice. When one person attacks another, fear is always at the bottom of it.

[Told of his experience with a vicious dog. This dog was kept chained by its owner. It was necessary for him to pass by this place each day to and from his home. One afternoon as he passed by, the dog in some way got loose, and came rushing madly up to him. He very calmly and lovingly said to the dog, "Why, you aren't afraid." Immediately the dog turned and walked away.]

It is always fear that makes men and nations fight each other. Fear is the primal cause of all evil; there is no evil in this world that doesn't spring from fear and ignorance. Ignorance is a state of fear. Divine wisdom makes you unafraid. Fear is ignorance of God, or good.

Forget people and handle fear as a generic claim without personality. Never attach any form of error to any person. The basic error is mortal mind; and to say there is no mortal mind, is just like declaring there is no fear.

It is always necessary to handle fear. Pain is always fear. All there is to hate is fear. There is nothing to limitation but fear. Mortal mind is fear, and fears anything and everything. Not only that, but the things it fears are of its own images and false beliefs. They do not exist. A thief is afraid. A liar is always afraid. The drunkard should always be treated for cowardice. That would also apply to other forms of vice. The man who drinks or uses drugs is trying to brace up some weakness in his character, something he is not always aware of. Never condemn him, but heal him. Rebuke the error and not the man.

It makes no difference how much fear there is in the patient, or in yourself in belief. Truth is greater than all the fear associated with the case, and sustains the activity of the Christ and the healing power of Christian Science in spite of fear. Handle fear in every case and you will be a successful worker in the most important work in the world.

Another point: Be very careful in talking to your patient that you do not ask questions that create fear. There is only one infinite Mind. You cannot possess any other. Fear is no part of that Mind, and no part of the understanding of that Mind. If one has the slightest understanding of Truth, that understanding of Truth is more powerful than all of the fear of the human race in a given case.

God is responsible for your understanding of Truth. When God created man, He assumed full responsibility for him. The divine Mind could never abandon its divine ideas. Without ideas, it would cease to be Mind; therefore fear isn't anything that anyone can possess. Nothing but harmony, health, love, and success are real; so in the light of all that is real and true, one never has any occasion to be afraid.

If you encounter fear on a case, know that it doesn't matter. Fear cannot do a thing, so it makes no difference if you are afraid or not. You can accomplish your purpose and make your demonstration even if you are afraid. You can approach your problem with the knowledge that God will always protect you. Keep marching on, knowing the Truth, if your knees are shaking. [Told about man calling Mr. Young once when he had a seemingly bad contagious case and his knees were shaking. Mr. Young said, "Your mind is not in your knees."]

You should in some cases handle the claim that man is unconsciously afraid, because there is a belief that unconscious conditions form the phenomena of mortal mind, and that these subconscious beliefs are to be feared, that they can express themselves after their mortal mind nature. This is the substratum of mortal mind, and it is nothing to fear.

Our materiality is the only thing subject to affliction, and materiality is mortal mind, and there is no mortal mind and no matter. Spiritual existence is all there is. The claim of fear is without original cause, without natural or derived existence. It is no part of Mind or being, forms no part of body, consciousness, or estate. It never existed in Mind, in Truth, or in belief, therefore it does not exist at all. If you know that, just know that your knowing extends to all the phenomena you are cognizant of, and you will make your demonstration over fear. There is no fear, however seemingly great, that can stand before the least understanding of the power of God; and you can prove this any time you want to.

Science and Health 410:29-30

Jesus

Jesus used the title *Christ*, and it became part of his name. So closely did Jesus identify himself with the Christ that he knew himself to be the Messiah. The man Jesus was a human conception. Mary's conception was not wholly immaculate for she was material in spite of her purity. The Roman Catholic dogma is that Mary was of an immaculate conception. In order to be the mother of God, they had to make Mary immaculate. Mary gave Jesus his state of materiality. The conception of Mary was wonderful, and showed the extraordinary purity of Mary.

Jesus, from the very first, knew his birth had equipped him in a special way to demonstrate the Christ. He seemed to sink very low at the crucifixion and cried out. That was the human sense. He refused wine and myrrh to ease his suffering. One Bible translation says he seemed to be free from pain. To material sense, Jesus seemed to die, but he never got to that point. The mission of Jesus was to demonstrate Life. The disciples became a different set of men after the resurrection.

Science and Health 39:13-14; 44:9; 75:12
Unity of Good 62:18-26

We should never admit that anybody has ever died. Jesus always spoke of death as sleep. If you do not submit to the lie, you will not be taken in by it. Know that Life is immortal and belief in death a dream. Error claims to exist, so there is need for a savior. Christ is Truth in its saving aspect.

Science and Health 230:4-10; 285:27-31;
   332:9-22; 473:10-12;
   496:15-19; 583:10-11
Miscellany 262:6-17

Message to The Mother Church of 1901 8:7-10
(next page)

The mission of Christ Jesus has been sadly perverted, making his death the central point of his life. You must cease to think of the word *Jesus* when you use the word *Christ*. Jesus was the man; Christ was what he knew. The divine Christ is the truth about everything. Christ is just as divine when you know it, as when Jesus knew it. Jesus did nothing but demonstrate the Christ. Not what he appeared to be, but what he knew, was what he always referred to as himself. You cannot separate Christ from God, and you cannot separate Christ from man.

You need not have a false sense of humility that would deny the Christ just because it happens to be your own thought; but on the other hand glorify the Christ in your understanding; it is your divine selfhood.

When you treat, do not be afraid. Assume all the rights and prerogatives of divine Mind. Think as Mind, and you will demonstrate the Christ. To know this great and comforting thing, is the Saviour under all circumstances, at all times, and everywhere.

The consciousness of the creator and man, right where you are thinking, is where it is taking place; it is there that the Christ heals; and it is there that the Christ comes to the human being and transforms his life. All the way the Redeemer is the Christ, is the oneness, the unity, the revelation of the perfection of man. All the way and forever is the pure intelligence of Deity, expressing and unfolding itself as the divine man.

Accidents

The name for every accident that ever happened, is *animal magnetism*. Animal magnetism is the name of something that never happened. The treatment is *God*. No matter what the appearance, *it never happened*. You will not do much good unless you stand and know that. All the incidents of true existence are provided for in infinite Mind, and they are always harmonious, and there are no accidents.

There never can be an accident or injury in the universe of Spirit; and your treatment destroys the belief that there can be a secondary result from the belief of accident, for it never happened and can have no effect. You will have to have enough understanding to substitute what you know for what they believe.

If you have a patient who comes to you with missing organs or mutilations from operations or accidents, handle hypnotism, because the patient thinks something has happened. It makes no difference what the claim is, there is no matter to it, and no mind and no being, and it never happened to anybody, even in belief. Always deny the accidents you see in the newspaper. It is always wise in case of an accident to handle internal injury. They will probably think it, even if they never say it: "Well, you never know, he might be hurt inside." *But we know.*

Life

Never record ages, and never gossip about the age of anyone, because this anticipates the claim of death, instead of handling it. Handle the belief of death everyday, and in your treatments deny that anybody or anything ever died. There is no death. Nobody ever died; nobody is ever going to die, and nobody is dying now. We cannot hold in belief the thought that the patient or any other person must die sometime, for that is not Christian Science. Not one idea of God can die, for if anyone could die, creation would collapse.

The claim that living creatures can get into the body and produce death, must be met, not as germs or microbes, but as mere belief in mental suggestion. You handle this claim when you know that Life is infinite, continuous, immutable, immortal, complete and harmonious.

There is no death in Life, no death for Life, no death to

Life, no death anywhere, for Life is God, and God is all. There is no provision of any kind for death, or what is called passing on, or any seeming death, any more than there is for sin and disease. Be sure that you understand this.

There is too much expectancy among Christian Scientists that passing on might be expected in some cases. But why? The suggestion that there is any relief, anything good or proper in the passing on of any person, is old theology, and is based on an utter misconception of God and man. It is unscientific, unchristian, and untrue. Principle is the Life of everything that lives or anything that seems to live, of everything that thinks or of anything that seems to think. The only Life or existence of anything or anybody that seems to be conscious or unconscious, is the one divine Principle that is never afraid and never dies.

Treatment cannot include the possibility of seeming death, remote or otherwise. For that reason, we should be particularly careful about accepting the belief of old age, either for ourselves or others. One of the commonest habits of the human being is to guess or surmise the age of all the people he meets. This is a sort of reciprocal malpractice that works evil for all concerned.

If the thought of any person's age comes to you, handle that thought as the suggestion of death, for according to mortal mind it is an unavoidable experience. Utterly refuse to take part in that claim. There is only one kind of life, and that is immortal life. It knows no age and never dies. We must continually oppose all theories, thoughts and experiences, that claim otherwise. The very fact that you can think involves you in the inevitable, great and final fact that Mind, God, Life, is *Life*, is our Life, the only Life we need or can ever have. Life is not the result of something; it is the cause of all things.

Life is the first, the primary fact. Life is undisturbed, not interfered with, continuous, never ending. Every treatment must be maintained on that basis, no matter what the material belief or evidence may be. Never treat people as though they had to die someday; never think that a patient has to die someday. You cannot go with death in your thought and demonstrate Life.

As we perceive the discords of human life to be nothing, we meet them. You cannot do a thing to Life; it is infinite; it goes right on being Life, ever-living, ever-loving, in all of its manifestations. If one maintains the facts of Life, the perfection and completeness of being, in his treatments, and does not admit at all the belief that there is anything of death, he will bring forth man's immortality. That is the object of all treatment, to bring forth God's creation, not merely to heal the sick, for healing is incidental to the far greater work of bringing to light the divine creation and the evidence of it.

Everything you do in your practice must have Life in it, and must be Life. The moment that you begin to understand that Principle is Life, you are attaining immortality. Principle is changeless, undying perfection. When the entire belief of human or material consciousness is dissolved, the divine structure of spiritual consciousness remains; it is God; it is from everlasting to everlasting.

Spiritual consciousness precedes birth and goes right on after the belief of death. Jesus referred to preexistence when he said, "Father, glorify thou me with thine own self, with the glory which I had with thee before the world was."

To be carnally minded is death; all there is to death is to be carnally minded. In *Science and Health* we read, "Existence continues to be a belief of corporeal sense until the Science of being is reached. Error brings its own self-destruction both here and hereafter, for mortal mind creates its own physical conditions. Death will occur on the next plane of existence as on this, until the spiritual understanding of Life is reached. Then, and not until then, will it be demonstrated that 'the second death hath no power'."

It is not an exaggeration to say that the great majority of Christian Scientists believe in death much more than they believe in Life. We have all been so tempted, because so far as human existence is concerned, the only thing that seems sure is death. Without

47

Science, the whole human race says, "as sure as death;" and Christian Scientists take that on; and although they do not say it, they think it. The only thing that is certain is Life; get that fact today and make it real; if you don't get anything else, *get that.*

Life is the only thing that is certain in the universe. The scientific certainty is that there cannot be anything else but Life. Anything unlike Life is a scientific impossibility; it cannot be. It doesn't make any difference if all the evidence in human belief contradicts Science, the answer is: Life *is*, and there is no death.

It is not possible that Life could be inside of anything, for we can see from the standpoint of ordinary education that the manifestations of human life are greater than any human being can conceive; consequently even human life, so-called, is bigger than any human being; so from the standpoint of human observation, Life is not something that can be inside of anything such as a human body.

The fact that millions of people are alive, shows that life is not a thing inside the human body, but something far greater than the manifestation; and therefore it must be entirely outside of the human body. Anybody who thinks, or will think, has to see, beyond all possibility of doubt or denial, that Life *is*; and nobody can do anything to it; and that means that nothing can be introduced into the body of man that can kill either him or his body. It is important in treating patients to know that Life *is*, there is no death, and to know it so clearly that it prevents the belief in death. A good Christian Scientist is Science.

"The Life which I now live in the flesh I live by the faith of the Son of God, who loved me, and gave himself for me." (Gal 2:20) That is a highly metaphysical statement; it means that the Life I now live in the flesh is controlled by my understanding of the Christ.

My Life is God. You can never change that fact. You do not change any fact because you entertain a false belief about it. We think of death as a secondary claim, the result of disease; it is not that way at all; *the belief in death produces disease.*

Mortal mind starts out in death, although it claims to be life. Death is a mortal thing; that is why mortal mind exists as a claim; so it gets disease in order to accomplish death; but the primary claim is death. Disease does not produce death; death produces disease.

Life is cause and effect; Life has no beginning, no interruptions, and no ending. It doesn't do anything that could make it inharmonious. Life is the Life of everything in the universe. You have only one Life, and it is your Life this moment.

Man is linked by indestructible, spiritual bonds to his divine Principle, Mind. Man is the full expression of Mind, Mind expressing its ideas. God is infinite, supreme intelligence, including and controlling every expression of Life and intelligence. For God is not only creator, but the divine governing intelligence and substance of all right ideas. False sense tries to come in and say you began when you were born. You always were one with God. Individual man never had a beginning.

Age is something you will have to consider. Age is slow death. If anybody grows old, it means he will die. You don't have to believe this. There is no more age than there is death. Age is one of the most persistent *diseases* in human belief. People may get over anything, but they are sure to succumb to age, according to belief. Are you going to take part in it, or are you going to take part in the demonstration over it? It is not a question of years. Years haven't a thing to do with it. It is not in years, or of years. Eternity is all there is. Just the everlasting now; there is no time at all.

Life is inevitable; you cannot escape it, no matter what you do. Let what you know handle death. The understanding which is itself so alive that it could not possibly believe in anything contrary to its aliveness, will handle death. Enoch and Elijah were transformed, and they never saw death. The material sense of life is death. To be mortally or carnally minded is all there is to this claim.

Miscellaneous Writings 78:1 (only)

Science and Health 584:9-16; 429:17-18;
    522:10-11; 427:5-16;
    251:8-12; 187:27-32; 290:3-10
Miscellany 110:1-4
Miscellaneous Writings 78:1 (only); 168:9-10
Science and Health 584:9-16; 429:17-18;
    522:10-11; 427:5-6;
    251:8-12; 187:27-32; 290:3-10
Miscellany 110:1-4

Time and Age

The claim or belief of time in reference to demonstration, enters into our thought and seems to be a part of our problem. Time is not a reality.

It is helpful to see that there is no element of time in omnipresence and omnipotence, and omnipresence is the nature of all action. Omnipresence is omni-action, and it doesn't require time. The law of infinite perfection to its own creation, is immediate in all its characteristics and does not take time, does not take space, is not restricted; it is simply omnipresence.

Mrs. Eddy says never record ages. Age should be and, when properly understood, is more full of power, wisdom and victory than youth. Mortal existence is a constant experiment. Spiritual life demonstrates unswerving Principle more fully and perfectly everyday.

Instead of losing one's faculties with the passing of years, as one sees God more clearly, his activity increases, his spiritual sense becomes more acute, his intelligence and perception are greater. There can never come a time when God's man can or must go downhill; onward and upward through all eternity his way must be.

There is no time; this is the time it has always been, last week, last year, a hundred years ago — it makes no difference which, because they are all the same. Even while we speak of the present moment, it is gone. This shows the unreality of time.

There is no before or after; nothing is a minute old, or a day, or a week, or a year, so now is exactly our age. We cannot be younger or older than now. Time has nothing to do with it or you. The ideas of Soul can never grow old. Hopeless, apathetic, depressed or vicious thinking makes for age, while enthusiasm, hope, love of humanity and spontaneity will keep us always young.

When we lift our consciousness into the spiritual realm, fixing our thoughts on the glorious, fadeless, undying present realities of the universe filled with ideas that are ever new, our whole being becomes rejuvenated, and we are refreshed and inspired by the everlasting truth of being.

Soul

The human mind is a seeming mingling and commingling, but only seemingly.

Unity of Good 37:17-2
Science and Health 95:31-5 (begin with spiritual);
    209:31-32; 60:29; 298:13-15; 359:14-17;
    481:7-9; 505:20-7; 596:1-2

The one who is demonstrating Soul will not seek to do it, but the beauty of his Soul will be manifested in his surroundings. Soul particularly stands for the things that beautify human experience, and make life more enjoyable. Soul is a word that signifies beauty, happiness, harmony, peace, and so on. Soul indicates a higher attainment of Science than Mind. Mind signifies reasoning faculties. Soul is the spontaneity of knowing without process. Soul is the substance of all beauty, the Principle, the activity, the law, of all that is beautiful. It is the impulsion of all true expression. Man is a state of revelation spontaneously showing forth Soul.

He who believes that he has a soul in his body, will have to get rid of that belief; there is nothing to that at all. There is only one Spirit, one Soul, and that is God. Soul is the divine Mind, and it is that particular quality of infinity that expresses itself in infinite beauty and grandeur throughout creation.

Soul is all there is to music and the arts. Everything that is beautiful, noble and grand, has its origin in Soul, in divine Mind. Human emotion is not altogether a quality to be avoided. Sometimes emotional people are much more scientific. If a person gets rid of his fear, and his human emotions are redeemed by Soul, he will become very intuitive; and often he will have a very clear perception and wisdom that will be sufficient to heal cases quickly, when a quality less loving and beautiful will fail to see the truth.

Soul is the spontaneous nature of man, the epitome of natural knowing. Soul is true inspiration. As you advance in the Science of Soul, you will see beauty where you never saw it before. A Christian Scientist attains his dominion in the proportion that he seeks not the image and likeness, but the original. In that original which is in Principle, Soul resides and shines in full effulgence, in all comeliness, originality, receptivity, beauty and joy. The fact is, you cannot demonstrate the kingdom of heaven unless you demonstrate beauty and joy in everything.

There is not an ugly thing in heaven; not one idea could ever show forth anything less than infinite Soul, which means infinite beauty and joy. We will never come into an experience where we cannot see and appreciate beauty by thinking in spiritual sense. The fact is that beauty and harmony accumulate and are more desirable and abiding than at present, because the kingdom of heaven is the kingdom of beauty.

Be sure that the kingdom of heaven is the kingdom of beauty. We need not think we can ignore the beauty of what we call the material world. The beauty is not material. We associate matter with beauty, but the beauty is eternal; and eternality will appear in the measure that we cease to associate matter and personality with beauty. These characteristics are not mere qualities; they belong to Being; they belong to man; they are Soul.

"Mystery, miracle, sin and death will disappear when it become fairly understood that the divine Mind controls man and man has no Mind but God." (*Science and Health* 319:17-20) Thus the connecting link between divinity and humanity is seen to be your scientific, right thinking; and this right thinking is not gained by secondary reflection, but by expressing the original, by thinking as Mind; and you do not have to wait to do it.

Heart

At a recent meeting of the American Medical Association, Dr. Mayo announced a decision by eminent physicians to the effect that heart conditions are due entirely to the emotional state. Heart disease will be healed in the measure that the practitioner knows that the heart is eternal and perfect. Heart can never be touched, affected, or inflamed with anything that would make it abnormal. There is only one heart, perfect as Mind, or Spirit.

Handle the belief of medical law. There is no enlargement to an infinite idea; nobody's heart is enlarged. For so-called leaky valve, know that blood is not a fluid; it is thought, and what a man knows cannot be lost through a belief. There is no leakage in infinity, and you must establish that as a law to that belief.

There is one heart; and when you find that divine heart, you will never have any palpitation. You do not live because your heart is beating; your heart is beating because you are alive. Life beats the heart, and life is eternal.

Your knowing that the heart is all right, is stronger than the universal belief which asserts itself as a law that there is something the matter with anyone's heart. Handle fear, and demonstrate what Life really is. When you establish the divine heart, the one we all have, you will see that there is one Life; and that Life is the impulsion of every idea; then the heart will not over-beat, under-beat, or fail to beat.

Arthritis

God, infinite good, is the only Mind, and the only substance of all right ideas. Every idea is the perfect expression of the one infinite cause. Every idea is governed, controlled, and sustained by the divine will, and has the same consciousness of perfection. God not only governs, but is the action of man; and the action of man expresses God.

God is Mind, Spirit, Life, Truth, Love, the substance of all being and the life of man, the one self-existent entity expressing Himself forever in perfection and completeness. Man is the perfection of all being expressed, and his identity is maintained in divine peace and harmony. He is not subject to sin, sickness and death. He is co-existent with God, the divine Principle, in which he has his being; and the law to that man is a law of continuity, joy and harmony; and that law is inviolate. His substance is not subject to inflammation, infection, friction, or pain.

There is no fear or mesmerism that can impair man's ability to use his joints as a normal activity of the human body. There is no arthritis. Arthritis is the name of a nameless lie, a name that means nothing because it is nothing to infinity. There is no substance that can manifest this belief, for all substance is Spirit.

In infinity, there is no law under which that belief can operate; and this treatment is a law of removal and complete obliteration to this belief, and a law of perfection and harmonious action to man. There is no cause of disease, no law of disease, no substance in which this claim can appear. In any treatment know this: that there is no cause, no law, and no substance in which such a belief can appear.

Malpractice

According to human belief, each person has a mind of his own; but it is nothing but the dumping ground for centuries of false belief. It is the kind of mind that keeps him involved in all sorts of fears and thoughts more or less unlike God. We cannot depend upon the means and methods of ordinary thought. We must look to the infinite wisdom of Mind to supply us with sufficient wisdom to meet every seeming condition that may arise in human belief. We cannot accept the views of those who believe in the reality of evil. In all the affairs of human life, we need to recognize the naturalness and infallibility of divine wisdom.

The knowledge of God, the infinite Truth, is exactly the same knowledge now as it was in the time of Jesus. The same ideas that made him the Christ, makes us Christians. The same ideas which constituted his enlightenment, should be the incentive and the governing power in our lives.

For that reason, a human being who is interested in Christian Science should walk, talk, carry on his business and even breathe and digest his food through the demonstration of Mind.

Man has all that God has, and everything about him is indestructible and exists at the standpoint of imperishable entity. No mindless, destructive force can trespass on the identity that God has made His own expression.

Insist upon knowing yourself as God knows you — the real man, the real you. Realize that God has created man in His own image and likeness, unlimited, harmonious, indestructible, pure and perfect, and that individual man will never cease to exist, to express good, because God must have expression, must be manifested to verify His own existence, and man is this expression.

Recognize the grandeur and naturalness of right ideas, also the infinite range of your thought when it expresses divine Principle; and when you think, instead of thinking from a material basis in a material world, let your thought embrace the universe.

Science and Health 264:9-10,15-20; 265:10-15

Every claim of sin and disease is but a phase of malpractice. Everything that appears in the way of resistance to Truth is malpractice. That people, places, things, organizations, events, are involved in wrong practice, should not mislead us. None of these things should make us lose sight of the fact that mortal mind is the culprit, the basic error. We must not make the mistake of putting malpractice into people, places, or things, simply because mortal mind suggests that the error is a person with the intention of involving us in a personal controversy.

If one manifests a belief of malpractice, he is the worst victim of that belief. The hater gets all the hate, and this is a good thing to remember. We must be especially alert to the phase of malpractice that calls itself a personality or personal mind, and even calls itself a Christian Scientist, and sometimes uses the deceptive art of correct statement together with protests of love and loyalty, with the purpose of deceiving Christian Scientists and destroying their demonstrable understanding of Science.

Some people imagine they are having trouble because they are doing good. Do not believe that. They will come and say, or at least they will think, that because they are doing good, they have to meet this awful error. It did not hurt them to meet the error, and it was not because they were doing good that they had to meet it, but because they were not doing good enough.

If your understanding or realization is one with God, is really God, God-with-us, you will not have much trouble, because you will recognize and offset the claim before it has a chance to do anything to you. There is a claim of malpractice, but remember it is a *claim* and nothing else.

Always be ready to make a fearless analysis of malpractice, because you have the ability, power and intelligence to handle its every suggestion; and you must never doubt that power and understanding to *destroy the belief with unfailing certainty*. Our work is to know the facts of divine Science so well that we can handle the beliefs of malpractice with perfect assurance. Don't make a metaphysical devil out of malpractice. Learn to be calm, peaceful and serene under all circumstances, because that is the way to hold error in check. Be triumphant, victorious, before you start to handle the claim of malpractice. Get that certain strength born of God and exercise it. It is yours for the taking at any time, and its dominion is absolutely invincible.

In treating any phase of malpractice, you must know that evil thoughts cannot reach beyond their own evil mentality — which is nothing but mortal mind — and *there is no mortal mind*. You are not in the realm where that belief claims to operate. You are "hid with Christ in God," with Truth in divine Love, as our Leader says. You do not have to fight malpractice, but you cannot ignore the claim. Know there is no mortal mind to assert itself as malpractice. Know there is no mortal mind. *All is infinite Mind & its manifestation*

It is sometimes necessary to seem to recognize the malpractitioner. Condemn the error, but not the person. Both the malpractitioner and the malpractice are nothing but belief, and are unreal. It is all a lie, a false claim without place, space, or occupancy. All correct handling of malpractice consists of unfailing recognition of it as unreal. No kind of evil thought can reach you, if you know that you cannot be made to respond to mental suggestion. There has to be a bridge, and if there isn't, there will be no malpractice.

Try not to malpractice. I ask you to be super-diligent about this. Avoid all gossip, even good gossip. "Have you heard about Mrs. So-and-So? Of course, it isn't true, but . . . " You could not have a more perfect defense against malpractice than to never indulge in gossip in any form. That is the best possible protection. We do not argue against malpractice for the purpose of resisting something, but only to find out that it is nothing, and to prove its nothingness.

It is essential to recognize that mortal mind says there are malpractitioners, but the claim is always malpractice, and malpractice is nothing. It has no cause, no origin, no being, no substance, no soul, no life, no subject, no object, no mentality, and no system; it has no mind or capacity to think; it has no education, never did anything, is not doing anything now, never had a first practitioner, has none now, and it is nothing. Handle the claim of mental mal-practice intelligently, with confidence, and great dominion — and not so much as if it were real. Handle it as God would. God is not afraid of it. Don't be soft; that sort of person is just putty in the hands of schemers.

Love is Principle. Stand for that. Mental malpractice is suggestion. We know there is no thought transference in Truth be-cause there is but one consciousness; and man reflects this one consciousness and can never be misinformed about anything, but always knows perfectly, clearly and correctly.

The correct handling of malpractice, is the knowing that you can handle it — not a feeling that you have to argue with it. The fear of malpractice is about all there is to malpractice; and if you can absolutely obliterate the fear by knowing it is untrue and impossible, the claim will disappear. However, if you can't get rid of your fear, just know that fear cannot do a thing, and it doesn't make any difference if you are afraid or not. God is not afraid, and your fear cannot make malpractice real.

We cannot ignore the claim that there are intentional ef-forts to malpractice, but you must know they are confined to their own realm of belief. There is no thought transference, no thought projection, no belief that one mortal mind can control another or have influence over it. God, the one Mind, governs, and is the only power, Mind, or presence. Sometimes malpractice is supposed to affect one's food, but deny that. A Christian Scientist does not catch cold — it is malpractice; he never has indigestion — it is malpractice; if he has a pain in the joints, it is malpractice; if his eyes fail, it is malpractice; if he falls and he knows it is malpractice (but there is no malpractice), he will never strike the ground.

There must be no doubt about the power of Truth — just know. Any sense of doubt is the devil himself. Make mental mal-practice unreal. Mortal mind has always made it real, and you are to put Christian Science into operation to handle this claim.

You cannot believe in malpractice if you believe in one

Mind. Malpractice is not a cause of pain, and the claim is not the effect of malpractice; it *is* malpractice. There is a distinction between animal magnetism and mental malpractice. Animal magnetism is the specific term designating the activity of mortal mind, a general term covering everything erroneous. Mental malpractice is the specific term Mrs. Eddy uses to designate certain conditions of thought that are more or less aggressively at work. Malpractice and mental suggestion are synonymous.

Mrs. Eddy says mental malpractice is a bland denial of Truth. She does not say it is always malicious or aggressive. The distinction as to the various phases of animal magnetism is not so closely drawn. They overlap each other, and it is not absolutely essential that you should say specifically whether malpractice is educated, ignorant, or malicious; because any belief of a power opposed to God is animal magnetism.

You cannot just slide along and never handle error. You are either handling it, or you are not handling it. It would be a great mistake for you to devote all of your time to the handling of animal magnetism and malpractice. Devote your time to knowing God, and that will handle animal magnetism.

There are times when a Christian Scientist is safer if he just recognizes that there is no opposition to what he knows, to the only system based on Life. The supposititious opposition is mortal mind, a system based on death. You couldn't possibly handle error and be unhappy. In fact, unhappiness will indicate that error is not being taken care of.

Never use a word that by any possible chance might give reality to malpractice. Evil is nothing; it has no place in God's creation; therefore it must go out before the law of God, which is the only law operating. Always keep error classified as nothingness.

When human opinion seems to have much to say about a case that is not getting along, we should treat the claim that this case is not getting along as it should, for that is the claim. You must know that Christian Science cannot be robbed of its power through weight of human opinion. The only treatment that works, is pure Christian Science; and this annuls the seeming power or effect of malpractice. It is a claim of power that does not exist.

Practically without exception, the return of an old belief, relapse, or fluctuation, must be handled as so-called laws of *materia medica*. This is pure malpractice, and purely theoretical.

The term animal magnetism may be used interchangeably with mortal mind; there isn't any difference. Never make the mistake of handling animal magnetism as a fact. Never condemn anyone, and do not let anyone condemn you.

Beliefs of pride, jealousy, envy and resentment, must not be ignored, but handled as animal magnetism. You will handle animal magnetism with unswerving success if you handle it as mere belief or illusion, and keep it there. If anyone says that animal magnetism exists, he is not a Christian Scientist. Some people are foolish on that subject.

Your understanding of Christian Science need not be disturbed because you are taking cognizance of a claim that is unlike your understanding. It has been said that the average Christian Scientist is not doing his daily protective work as it should be done, especially the men. To fail to protect yourself, is one of the most flagrant errors you could name. Do your daily protective work, because it is very important. Declare everyday that there are no accidents, that health is normal and that nothing can change it, that there is no necessity to resort to material means, that man's home is in the divine consciousness, and that all is Love, harmony, peace, protection, and care, without measure or limitation.

Scientific Attitude toward Error

There are those who neglect to handle animal magnetism, and also those who make too much of it. We are living in a day when animal magnetism is very subtle.

Science and Health 446:31-32; 252:8-14;
    447:20-22; 542:19-26

Animal Magnetism Defined

Science and Health 472:13-19; 71:1-4; 92:21-31; 269:3-8
Miscellaneous Writings 45:21-9; 346:6-21
Christian Healing 9:21-12
Message for 1901 14:25-9
Science and Health 103:18-24; 484: 21-24;
    102:16-23; 484:6-20;
    485:2-5; 486:23-2; 104:13-18
Manual of The Mother Church: Article VIII: Section 6
Miscellaneous Writings 31:2-2 (next page)
Miscellany 146:23-32

Malpractice may be regarded in three ways: (1) All unspirit-ual thinking. (2) Any thought of evil entertained by one who knows the difference between good and evil. That, of course, is worse because he knows better. (3) Where evil thoughts are held and intentionally directed to do harm. This is malicious.

There are two points to remember:

> 1. *Do not fail to see the claim of malpractice.*
> 2. *Do not fail to handle it as nothing.*

There is no malpractice in Truth; and when you see this, you are absolutely immune from the claim. Have no fear about it at all. If a Christian Scientist says he is sick or feeling badly, he is malpracticing on himself.

Science and Health 461: 16-30; 469:12-17

61

Be careful never to sow one seed in your patient's thought that would make evil real. Stick to the fact that one Mind alone is active; if the claim of evil doesn't convince you, it cannot touch you. Never admit that evil has any power and intelligence; never, never let it become your thought; and you will be happy, and useful.

Science and Health 103:29-31; 104:1-2,
(begin "scientific")

Handling Animal Magnetism

Science and Health 92:21-25; 207:2-14;
357:7-19; 346:15-16;
447:24-29; 366:22-29; 218:24-26; 35:30 (only)

There is no such thing as an unforgivable sin; there is no such thing as an incurable disease; and there is no such thing as too late.

Science and Health 475:2-4

Joy is the only bucket that will draw water from the wells of salvation.

Science and Health 566:29-13

The real man has no contest. Most of us are like Michael and have contests, but our Michael should be backed up by Gabriel. Quiet knowing is sometimes doing much more than could otherwise be accomplished. There is a great deal of the Gabriel in the quiet, strong worker.

Aggressive malpractice, or aggressive mental suggestion, claims to work through mental telepathy sometimes. You handle that by knowing that the divine Mind is always present, and that only God's thoughts pass to man. If you believe that a person who has done something wrong must suffer, that is malpractice.

You must demonstrate great love and compassion in healing cases. Truth and Love uncover error. Always think of Love being present at the uncovering. Never be harsh. You may have to warn them lovingly. It may be that the only thing that is the matter, is that the poor sufferer thinks he is under penalty; and the penalty ends with the belief.

Science and Health 223:28-31; 277:19-23;
　　　419:1-3; 385:11-14;
Message for 1901 13:22-3

Animal magnetism accepts all of the good statements about the divine ideas. It will admit the real man is harmonious and perfect; but it claims that in belief man is having a hard time; so you will have to know that malpractice cannot operate even in belief.

Sometimes one will have a suggestion, or a sense, that evil is about to happen. Then is the time to stop it. Fear of the devil is all there is to the devil. The belief that error has a believer is the claim. The need is never to be afraid or alarmed at an appearance that is only a belief. Obliterate that human concept with the divine realization. Never talk about the claim of malpractice or animal magnetism. Never ever think of it as if it had real existence.

Treatment

The real man being spiritual, is not subject to any false claim of old theology, *materia medica*, physics or hygiene, because they are without Life, Truth, power or intelligence to claim God's idea for any purpose. They have no power to establish themselves in the consciousness of man, the conscious idea whose activity and power are in Truth. Truth, Life and Love are a law of annihilation and elimination to all that is untrue and unlike God.

The belief of Life, Truth or intelligence in matter, is a false claim in all its ramifications. It has no substance, no origin. It is not mind. It has no law; and as a false claim of mortal mind, it is false in everything that could claim to be, and cannot have any claim of activity in any case we are treating. It cannot create a single thought that can operate in Christian Science. It cannot create a channel or avenue through which to act.

Know

Mental malpractice cannot operate through envy, jealousy, fear, revenge, hate, pride, ambition, passion or appetite, or through laws of belief in *materia medica*, or through laws of hypnotism, mesmerism, suggestion, argument, poison or drugs.

No mortal mind can enter, direct, or read my thoughts. My thoughts cannot be picked or found out by any process of clairvoyance, and this treatment destroys all such beliefs. I cannot be treated unscientifically.

Mortal mind has no method or will; it cannot assert itself as will, wish, desire, prophecy, pride, ambition, deceit, smartness — or in any way at all. Animal magnetism has no being, presence, power, action, substance, law, entity, mind, or intelligence; it is absolutely nothing, without existence.

Mortal mind cannot operate consciously or unconsciously, directly or indirectly, maliciously or at all. It cannot argue depression, suppression or destruction in any way. It is a false claim without any being; and this treatment annuls it, wipes it out, so that it will never have any seeming power or influence.

There is no mortal mind to interfere with the boundless expression of man's unity with God in the abundance of good. Mind, God, the infinite intelligence of the universe, the Life of all being, infinite Truth, and Love, the I AM of all true being, the substance of all ideas, the one self-existent cause of all that really exists, is forever expressing itself as the activity and impulsion of its perfect embodiment, man and the universe.

64

The divine Mind and idea are *one in substance, one in action, one in being.* This infinite unity of Mind and idea, is all there is. There is no mind apart from I AM, no substance, no law, no holiness, no action, no condition or being, apart from harmony and perfection. "All is infinite Mind and its infinite manifestation." (*Science and Health* 468:10-11)

Mortal mind is a false belief, an impossible falsehood, absolutely nothing; and animal magnetism, as a phase of this nothingness, has no origin, no cause, no entity, no being, no substance, no law, and no derived power or law by which, or through which, this false belief of a mind apart from God can operate to interfere with the divine action of Christian Science practice.

There is no condition, no circumstance, event or occasion, by which the belief of animal magnetism can interfere with or prevent the successful operation of Christian Science practice.

There is no condition, no circumstance, event or occasion, by which the belief of animal magnetism can interfere with or prevent the successful operation of Christian Science treatment.

Mental malpractice cannot hide the Truth. There is no law of mental malpractice that can prevent a Christian Science treatment from operating and establishing the evidence of health and peace in human consciousness, and obliterating from that consciousness every afflicting belief. The law of divine Being is the law of the treatment, its presence, its power, its energy, its enforcement, and its tangible force and substance.

That which is substance, is incapable of suffering, and so cannot suffer. Mind, God, Love, the harmonious law of perfection, is active in this treatment, and this treatment is operating in human thought and experience. This is the law to this case, and a law of annulment and extinction to the false belief of fear, sin, sickness and death.

The nature of law is omni-action, and its substance is the same as its source, which is Mind. Spiritual law is the only means through which divine Principle expresses itself. It is therefore never inoperative, never intermittent, never afflictive, never mortal, never annulled, never opposed, never reversed, never resisted; for every idea, organ, function, circumstance, or event, in creation spontaneously conforms to omniscience, and can have no consciousness of anything contrary thereto.

The belief of mental malpractice is a mindless, lawless falsehood. It cannot act, be or do. It cannot assert itself in belief as the suggestion of insidious forms of disease or sin. It cannot claim to be my experience or any part of my mind, my body, my home, my business, my environment, or my life; it cannot claim to act in belief, or at all.

The belief of mental malpractice cannot and does not possess or suggest power or influence. It cannot assert itself in my thought or in any other way dethrone the Christ-power in healing, interfere with the activity of this treatment, delay its results, prevent it from healing, or cause fluctuations or reversals.

The claim of mental suggestion is no part of the Mind that is God, and no part of the consciousness that is man, and no part of the patient who has asked for Christian Science treatment. The picture of sin, disease or discord is but mental suggestion; it does not, nor can it, occupy my thought or attention, form any part of my imagination, or be entertained or retained in my consciousness, nor in any way, by any means whatsoever, interfere with or delay my realization of its utter nothingness.

Errors about Man

1. That he is separated from Principle. This error is the point of departure from all spiritual growth.

2. That he is not entirely separate from error.

3. That he is composed of contrary qualities, good and evil, truth and error.

4. That he is divided into human beings.

5. That he is divided into sexes.

6. That he is limited in every aspect or particular.

7. That he is not perfect in all respects.

8. That he is different now from what he was or will be. (*Science and Health* 470:32-5)

9. That he is governed by something other than divine Principle.

10. That he is governed by his nerves, his liver, his stomach, or some organ of the body. Man is governed by God's law, by Principle's law. We are not governed by nerves, but by God. It is tragic how much the human being thinks matter is governing him!

11. That man is subject to chance, heredity, environment, the conduct or misconduct of other persons; that he is a creature of circumstance. These things never touch the real man. The only environment is the environment of divine Mind.

12. That he is competitive and not cooperative.

13. That he began with human birth.

14. That he develops from infancy to manhood, and then deteriorates.

15. That we have the fallacy that man dies. Mrs. Eddy points out that fear causes death. At every point of infinite space there is Life.

16. That he undergoes after death a final judgment which consigns him to heaven or hell. (*Science and Health* 291:28-32)

17. That he enters into a state called purgatory. This is a belief held by millions today. This is a great money-getter for the Roman Catholic church. The real man is always in heaven.

18. That he enters into a state of suspended life pending resurrection. Millions of people also believe this. Get the real body and it will take care of that.

19. That he does not fully reflect the divine Mind.

Church

The Christian Science Church, consisting of The Mother Church and the branch churches, is intended to humanly express the nature and law of the divine prototype, but the material organization is not that prototype. This organization with its buildings, and many departments, though doing good alone, is nevertheless composed of human elements. Mrs. Eddy says that she spiritually organized The Mother Church, but she does not say that The Mother Church is a spiritual organization.

A Christian Science church as presented to the human senses is a human belief. Sometimes it is an improved belief, but sometimes it isn't. At any event, it must be further improved; and the thing that improves it is the practice of Christian Science healing.

Everything else is subservient to this healing. Without the healing there would be no church. The foundation and superstructure of the church is the healing.

Jesus said the Sabbath was made for man and not man for the Sabbath. This is entirely true of the Church and all that constitutes the Christian Science movement. It was made for man.

It must be preserved and protected, and we must not, as Paul says, worship the creature instead of the creator. Roman Catholicism manifests the church rather than God. On the other hand, our movement, carried on by The Mother Church and the branches is the visible hope of mankind.

The spirit of revelation is still in human consciousness, and mental suggestion seeks to circumvent it. It is to the credit of Christian Scientists that they rarely respond to its suggestion. We have not outgrown the organization until we can heal the sick instantly, or so long as there is another organization opposed to our activity.

Christian Scientists are wise enough to recognize the claims that are incident to human organizations; and they see that our organization, though not faultless, is nevertheless serving the race through its healing and rejuvenating work. In this connection, it is highly important that Christian Scientists watch that they be not touched by the suggestion of criticism toward those who are carrying on the work in Boston and those who represent the work in the field. Let us give them the support of love, loyalty, and gratitude.

Nine-tenths of the church members are only members; one tenth are workers. Belonging to a church does not do anyone any good unless he is demonstrating the truth. It is not a question of time in being a good Christian Scientist. It is a matter of perception. A person might be a young Scientist and a very fine worker, or he might be in the movement forty years and be a very poor worker.

You should neither seek nor shirk church work. Do not err in either direction. Carefully avoid trying to have influence and power in the church or the church work. Get the kingdom of heaven in consciousness and you will have great power, but it will not personally get you any power.

Never seek church office; it is the last thing to do; but if it comes to you by demonstration, then do it; but do not seek it. It would be wrong, and you would not be happy, unless you were put into it by Principle. Eventually a Christian Science church will have to be demonstrated as a democratic church, in which all of the people or a majority are demonstrating the one Mind, each one governing himself through divine Principle, thereby in perfect harmony with his brother, not condemning anyone, only condemning and overcoming error, and demonstrating the divine church in his own consciousness.

In the metaphysical work of the church, whether you are in office or not, you ought to do something. There ought to be a sense of pure spirituality in church membership. One should feel: Why I am not in the church; the church is in me. All I know about it is all there is to church.

What do I know about it? I know that it is the structure of Truth and Love. I know it is that which rests upon and proceeds from divine Principle. I know that it is like the universe, a spiritual creation of God, and maintained in perfection and harmony, and forever unfolding as a divine idea.

Whenever something different than that presents itself to thought, what is it? Animal magnetism. It then seems to be an organization of people, many different minds, some of them good workers, most of them not workers at all; some of them hardly understanding the words *Christian Science*. All of that constitutes what is called a church. Now what are you going to do with it? Shall we take the evidence of the senses and go no further, or shall we find the divine idea and maintain it so clearly that our understanding helps change the belief?

Lots of Christian Scientists have been going along through life, and never had any occasion to have things said about them that were condemnatory. Lots of them have gone along very well and have never been called liars, never been called wicked, never been called vicious and sensual; and they come into Christian Science churches and begin to do excellent work among their fellow students; and these things happen to them for the first time. Sometimes, when you get into church work, if you go by the evidence, you would say that Christian Scientists were the worst people you ever saw; but you can't say that. Plenty of them are good and kind and noble. The thing to do is never to permit any false belief to find lodging in your consciousness for a single instant.

If your feelings get hurt, get rid of your feelings. We are here to demonstrate true knowledge.

In church or any other place, there is nothing more stultifying to intellect and morality than gossip. It is the role of Christian Science to arouse more love.

It is not right for churches, founded upon the rock, to fall into the hands of inexperienced or over-zealous people, or such management that they find themselves in debt. This sort of thing is not right, and ought not to happen.

Why does it occur? Because some very enthusiastic people

assume that because they say something, they have proved it. It is easy to say beautiful things, but a different thing to prove them.

In almost every church where there is a Board of Directors, you will find presently there is a little division. You will find Mrs. So-and-so, and maybe another Mrs. So-and-so lined up together. The tendency is that something comes up, and the Chairman hears about it, and he goes over to someone's house, and they talk it over and decide what to do. This is rank error.

It would be perfectly legitimate to telephone them all and say that such a thing has come up; please make it a part of your daily work, so we will have a demonstration. The thing that will take care of that will be consecrated action, and agreement of the Board of Directors never to talk over matters at home, never to talk over matters that relate to the Board of Directors to each other privately. Demonstrate the divine Mind in handling such matters.

To take part in this work is a splendid thing, but if a person is in business or so situated domestically that his time is taken up, and his business is of such a nature that it would not be possible to do church work, it would perhaps be wrong to be influenced to take church office if it took hours away from his business. He has to be careful that he is not handled by animal magnetism influencing him in the name of Love to do something wrong, because it would be wrong for him to neglect his business.

If he's satisfied from the standpoint of Principle that his reason is a correct and good one, he can say, "It is just impossible. I regret that I cannot do it." Never give a reason, because in some instances somebody might question the reason and it might come back to you; but if you never give a reason, you cannot be condemned for that reason. There is human wisdom necessary in church relationships. Scientists are always explaining things which don't require explanation. Take an office if you can, and do the work well. If somebody doesn't like your work, just say, "I am sorry; glad you told me." Then just pass along and forget it. In all church dissension, it is Roman Catholicism at work, although it appears to be somebody in the church. You don't have to look for anything; just handle Roman Catholicism. They will attempt to find some characteristic in a person, and they will work on that as though mortal mind were working along a wall trying to find a weak spot to push through.

The only organization in the universe is that of Spirit, and any other claim of organization is a false claim without entity, being, power, influence, law, presence, or manifestation.

The claim that we call Roman Catholicism is that of material organization in the name of Spirit. It is a self-acknowledged state of weakness. It cannot and does not exist within or without a Christian Science organization to disrupt its members, or to interfere with its activities, or to dislodge its organization; it cannot take part in the organization, or influence any of its members to do anything contrary to divine Principle. Something like this is what you should do for your church everyday.

When Mrs. Eddy wrote the first edition of *Science and Health*, she did not believe in church organization. The first organization was not a success; the second was not altogether what she wanted; and finally in 1892 the present Church was organized and she provided the *Church Manual.* We must see the *Manual* for ourselves, and pray to understand it. The only thing that holds us together is the *Manual*, and nothing in that book ever needs to be changed to let us enter into the kingdom of heaven on earth.

Every person wants to rule or be ruled. It is so easy to have someone tell you what to do, and seemingly so hard to find out by your own work. Some rules are helpful, but everything in a church should be done by demonstration and not by rules. The *Manual* is the only thing we can depend upon. Unless one is daily affirming and realizing to the best of his ability the government of God, and conversely rejecting mortal mind and its so-called law, he is not a Christian Scientist, however much he may be doing unofficially, or officially, for the organization.

We must assert and maintain the divine law which governs

the real church, and also governs the organization by means of Christian Science; and because of our knowledge and demonstration of that Science, the kingdom of God is a present possibility; and the Science organization ought to be a human illustration of that kingdom.

The cause of Christian Science is far greater than any organization. It exists naturally through divine power and law. It is one with the true idea of church, and our church is universal and should be fostered and preserved only by gaining more spiritual power and by healing with more certainty and promptness.

When we first had the Lesson-Sermons as they are now, Mrs. Eddy saw there was a great need for every member of the organization to take part in the services. Practitioners used to say they went to church to do their work, and to treat their patients during the morning service. Mrs. Eddy did not think this was right, and so she said that the prayers in the Christian Science churches were to be for the congregations exclusively. You are not there to treat your patients; you are there to demonstrate the Lesson. That is your duty and privilege. You have as much work to do as does the First Reader. The most he can do is to know the Truth, and you shouldn't do less than that.

If the spiritual idea of church is with us, we will not have our church only on Wednesday and Sunday.

Find your wisdom in God, and not from your neighbor. We must get away from the sickly stuff some people call Christian Science. Establish the real Cause of Christian Science in place of what we seem to have now. Christian Science is divine law, the supreme wisdom of infinite Mind. Find the wisdom that constitutes the divine Mind and make it yours. There must come into human thought a divine standard in which man is found to be just like God.

We are called upon to make decisions everyday as to which of two courses is the best to take, when both are in the realm of belief; and we should use the best judgment we have, in a common sense way, and then go forward on our way unperturbed.

The Christian Science Church will fulfill the purpose of its Founder in proportion as Christian Scientists who constitute it are both awake and united in the demonstration of the one Mind, divine Principle, Love. The only thing that ever thinks is the one Mind. To the extent that anybody ever thought anything was true, it was because the divine Mind in some measure, whether he knew it or not, was reflected or expressed by him.

To the extent that anybody ever did anything that was right, it was the reflection of the divine Mind, whether he knew it or not; so anything good that was ever thought or done throughout the ages, even if it was not known, was Christian Science, just the same.

The divine Mind is constantly and instantly your available Mind. That God is all the prophets saw in an inspirational way. Old theology admitted it in an inspirational way, but Christian Science understands and demonstrates it scientifically.

In the meantime, each person must necessarily decide many questions for himself. His teacher cannot decide them; his church cannot decide them. The Board of Directors of The Mother Church cannot decide them. The questions are individual. A solution to them can only be found through searching one's heart in the light of profound study of our Leader's works. Common sense and common honesty guide a person in ordinary matters, and are not less available to us in fulfilling our duty to our Cause.

Now, the tendency of some in our organization is to go upon the assumption that something is being done, when nothing is being done at all; and this ought to be handled. You will find church members who are enthusiastic, and they will say, "Divine Love will do it; divine Love will give us everything." They will go deeply into debt, and still declare that they are going right on, that everything is lovely.

The fact is just this: That we are engaged in a *Science*, and not in the assumption that divine Love is going to do something. The fact is that divine Love never does a thing; it just simply *is*; and its eternal *isness* provides everything anybody could desire, and far more than anybody could ever think of in the way of blessings.

The whole question with any church member is not to be sentimental, but to be scientific; and you must take your stand. If the church is going to accomplish its mission, those who know how to work, and those who know what the Christ is, and those who think clearly, and those who are able to forget themselves through self-abnegation, will have to carry on this work.

If you have the enlightenment, you will have to stand in high places. You cannot avoid it, and you should not try to. It means you will have to stand, and stand when it is difficult to stand; and you will have to maintain what you understand, sometimes in the face of severe criticism.

There are things going on that will have to stop. The world has got to be taken care of, and those who know the Truth and have no human ambition but a sincere desire to do right, are the ones who will have to carry on this movement. Handle animal magnetism particularly in your church work.

The organization is what Roman Catholicism fears. It is well to recognize that the Roman Catholic organization, with its immense ramifications, is actively and ceaselessly engaged in the endeavor through mental work and otherwise to destroy the Christian Science movement.

A material organization, such as Roman Catholicism is, fears the manifestation or influence or power on the part of anything that is based on absolute right. That organization does not estimate Christian Science correctly in the slightest degree; and to be properly handled, we must see that their fear is older than human history, and is really due to a dim perception of its extinction. While we would not and should not ascribe anything like intelligence to error, we can recognize that its claim to intelligence is sufficient to enable it to perceive and dread the coming of the impersonal Christ.

There is only one church. That church does not include your consciousness, but is included *in* your consciousness. It does not govern man; man governs it; and because his government is that of righteousness, the church is the perfection of government. The perfect government is that of righteousness; the church is the perfection of government. The perfect demonstration of church government means, man governed by God, and therefore self-governed.

The government of God is purely spiritual and individual. In this way, a church organization shall ultimately exemplify a perfect human government; therefore we cannot over-estimate the value of real loyalty. We can be sure that the government is upon His shoulders — that is, that the divine idea reflects omniscience; and we can anticipate the prospect of the Christian Science movement freed from embarrassment within and opposition without, respected and honored of men, and carried forward and upward by the re-deemed, who have seen the folly of human desires, and have come legitimately into a large measure of divine possession through their demonstrable understanding of Christian Science.

Sunday School

The Sunday School is the greatest thing going on in our Church. Every church in the world that is building today, is absolutely wrong if it does not make provision for the Sunday School. It should not be necessary to hold Sunday School in the church building where the classes are so close together they interfere with each other. It is better to have another building.

The great question, however, is the teaching in the Sunday School. There isn't anything in the world so important as teaching in the way of church work. This is the greatest thing you can do, much greater than being a director or reader. It does not mean that the director's work is not great work; but if the children are going to be Christian Scientist, everything depends upon the teachers in the Sunday School. If the teaching is right, these children will stand always, through thick and thin.

The work for the class should always be impersonal and protective. You ought not have a child late, a child sick, a child indifferent. It is nice for you to get acquainted with them, if possible. Do not tell them to call upon you for help, because it is for them to choose whom they like; and they might think it would be necessary to call upon their teacher if you told them so. It would be misconstrued in spite of anything you could say. Divine Principle is divine influence. Teaching requires the best demonstration. It is a wonderful privilege, and our teachers ought to be the best on earth. It is the best opportunity we have in church to do good work.

The teaching ought to be wonderful, but often it isn't. The very best Scientists ought to be teaching Sunday School.

You are putting down a foundation for the children. You must explain the difference between old theology and Christian Science. Show them the difference between Truth and error. Show them that the Ten Commandments were given to a race of people who could not get any other laws.

Just to say, "Thou shalt not," does not make good children. Fear never made anybody good. Do not appoint someone who is a beginner in Science to teach little ones because it seems easy. Get the best and most experienced Scientists to teach little ones, because it is the hardest and most important work there is.

Teach the meanings of the words in the Ten Commandments and the "scientific statement of being." Exercise judgment and follow the *Manual* carefully. Do not teach old theology. Try to find a way to give the metaphysical meaning of the Ten Commandments. Do not give the children the idea that God punishes. Show them how all the Commandments correspond to the First Commandment. You are safe when you keep on the side of Love.

Rely on Mind. You will have to know that the divine Mind will instruct you to know what to say, and know that you will have the power of illustration in simple ways, that you can and do express and reflect divine intelligence, and that you cannot possibly say anything that is not in strict accordance with Christian Science.

It has been observed that many children, notwithstanding that they go to a Christian Science Sunday School, will have an intense feeling about a personal God. It is because the personal pronouns are used altogether too much in the teaching. It is hard for them to say He and mean Mind. All the time you must impersonalize the teaching so that they can see Principle, Mind, Love absolutely as a fact.

In teaching, one of the most important things is to find out if the child repeats the "scientific statement of being" in a rote manner. When you ask him what it means and he does not know, then what is the use of repeating it? He has to know what it means, and you will have to find a way to explain it to him. You will have to find a way to explain what the words mean.

It is your demonstration to find some simple means of teaching that will enable the children to understand what they say, and to get the significance of God and man. Occasionally the teaching is flying too high over their heads in far too many statements. Teaching anywhere, of anything, is a question of scientific pedagogy. It is just as scientific in Christian Science. It is more so, in fact. Be scientific in your pedagogy. Get so your teaching is in accordance with the highest and best standards of teaching and with the Christ Spirit, which is Truth and Love.

The first Commandment is the real one of the Ten. The others were given because the people could not understand the first; therefore they must be explained from the standpoint of the first, and in no other way.

Understanding what God is, will explain the first Commandment, and as the children understand it, they can see that God is Love and get rid of a person in their thought. Then, step by step, let the other Commandments be explained to them to the extent that you can explain them.

"Jealous God" means that God does not compromise with error. A watchful, loving God does not admit anything unlike Himself.

Of course, to explain some of the Commandments metaphysically is rather difficult, but do the best you can and go on. Get them to see that to be unkind, unloving, selfish or unjust, is to adulterate the Truth of Being. That will take care of that Commandment, and help them. You don't have to explain that in any other way, for you cannot expect them to understand a thing that the human race itself is not able to explain, even when they are grown up. If they get the idea of noble conduct and noble thought, they will get the meaning of the Ten Commandments.

When you have a class that is of an age that can study the Lesson, talk it over with them, and get them to talk. Make it a give and take. If a mistake is made, point it out in such a way that you do not offend the child. The thing is not to hurt the feelings of the child. The correction should be made in such a way as not to hurt them in the eyes of the members of the class.

In correcting statements in the Sunday School, it is sometimes far better to work around to it by a little explanation, or just ask the question, "Don't you think this?" and the student will probably make the correction himself. Then you have the real art of teaching, and it is a wonderful thing.

These children that are clamoring for admission have to be considered; and each case has to be considered on its own merits. There are cases when Roman Catholicism baptism does not mean a thing. Water sprinkled on a body does not do a thing to it. Don't give power to that stuff.

Here is the question: Whether Roman Catholicism influences exist, or if it has been destroyed through some understanding of Christian Science. Even if it has been believed in for years, it might be wiped out completely in Christian Science in ten minutes or less, because Christian Science is equal to that. You will have to use good judgment, and demonstrate wisdom and Love. For a Christian Scientist to be in a state of fear about Roman Catholicism, is not common sense. You are making nothing of error, or something of it.

Most of our trouble in church work is caused by Scientists getting to the point where they think they are humanly good. You cannot trust goodness, but you can trust God.

The world is not going to be saved by good people thinking there are bad people in it. Let every Christian Scientist prove himself a real Christian Scientist — modest,   sincere, and not seeking place or power. Roman Catholicism itself is the error and not the people. The decent ones are not making any trouble, but be very wise and keep your armor on.

Science and Health 24:4-10

Avoid self-interpreting the Bible. The following Bible Reference Books were recommended by the Metaphysical College:

1. American Version of the Bible
2. Twentieth Century New Testament
3. Weymouth Translation
4. Goodspeed New Testament
5. Moulton's Bible
6. Moffatt's Translation
7. Isaiah and the Minor Prophets,
          by George Adams Smith
8. Moffatt Introduction to the
          New Testament Literature
9. Historical Geography of the Holy Land
          by George Adams Smith
10. The Greatest English Classic, by McAffee
11. How to Know the Bible, by Hodges
12. The Story of Religion, by Smith
13. How We Got the Bible, by Smith
14. St. Paul's Life and Letters, by Smith
15. Harmony of the Gospels by Stevens and Butrons
Bible Concordances: Nelson's; Young's; Strong's

Bible Dictionaries: Oxford English (best); Hastings
(excellent)
New Standard (very good); Practical Standard (good)
Chamber's Twentieth Century (good)

Roman Catholicism

Every person who claims to be a Christian Scientist should be clear on this subject. We must get a sane and balanced view of this evil. Many erroneous beliefs are held about it all through the field. We cannot possibly ignore Roman Catholicism, and no alert Christian Scientist is doing so.

"A genuine Christian Scientist loves Protestant and Catholic, D.D. and M.D., — loves all who love God, good; and he loves his enemies." (*Miscellany* 4:14-16) This is the correct attitude to bring to your patients.

You will have to approach this subject with love in your heart. In this system many false beliefs are held, such as Jesus is God; Mary is the Mother of God; the Pope is the representative of God on earth. They believe that Roman Catholicism is God's special means of reaching and dealing with man, whereas the fact is that Christian Science is the universal religion proclaiming impersonal Truth.

In Roman Catholicism, the claim is that evil may be good; that evil may be done in order that good may come to the church; this especially is accepted as part of that system. They believe, therefore, that they need not necessarily keep faith with a Protestant. They claim to do what they please in the name of God.

The laity are distinctly different from the hierarchy. The laity are kept in ignorance; and among them are many decent people; but as you get nearer to Rome, you will find a complete and corrupt political organization. The hierarchy hold that anything they do in their interest is good.

"The Christianity that is merely of sects, the pulpit, and

fashionable society, is brief, but the Word of God abideth. Plato was a pagan; but no greater difference existed between his doctrines and those of Jesus, than today exists between Catholic and Protestant sects." (Miscellaneous *Writings* 111:21-25) There is a profound difference between Roman Catholicism and Protestantism. The Protestant clergymen have a different sense of good.

These people, Roman Catholics, are taught to take advantage of anything. The real teaching is this: To flatter this one and jolly that one. It is not an infrequent thing to hear a person say, "The priest in our town is very friendly toward Christian Science." Of course he is; that is the way he works. Be wise and don't fall for such deceit.

In belief, they are the greatest organization in the world; and they try to hold the human race in a grip that they will never give up. All of the systems that have been devised to overcome that claim have failed. Either the Roman Catholic organization has been able to overcome opposition from the outside, or failing in that, they have introduced on the inside some elements that have served to disintegrate it. That is the history of every effort that has been made to overthrow this organization which would keep the race in ignorance and mental slavery.

Something has to be done. So long as a human organization could not succeed, there had to be some concerted effort or endeavor that would rest upon a basis that could not be shaken. Mrs. Eddy established this Cause, the purpose of which is to overcome visible and invisible evil, and that work requires attention. But it is nothing to get excited about. Do not think that you have to devote all your time to talking about Roman Catholicism. Don't talk about it at all. Even in our church, say nothing. Keep still and saw wood.

Never talk about malpractice — absolutely never. Make no exceptions about this and you will be right. *But handle it. Handle it.* This work must be done by us, because we see the subtlety of the claim.

The priesthood are taught and trained in their schools to use mental power. They know how to use the human mind. Their teachers are so-called clever and able men. While they do not have the Inquisition openly, they have it mentally. They practice this mental power on their laity and in the confessional. Protestant Ireland has less fear of this thing than we in America. Don't make too much of this claim and talk of it all the time. It is nothing. They say that God, through the Pope, gives them power to forgive sins for money. Christian Science teaches sin is forgiven only when it is destroyed.

They operate very largely through fear, and often cause positive disaster in the homes of the ignorant laity. Some of the hierarchy are clever and so-called intelligent men, and their schools of philosophy are well equipped, but they know nothing of the divine Mind, and we have got them there. Because of this trained will power, they are the most single power of evil today. They are absolutely opposed to anything good. It is almost unbelievable. In fact, we wouldn't believe these things if we didn't know them to be true of that organization. They do not fear Protestants, but they fear Christian Scientists. They are afraid Christian Science will exterminate their religion, and it will.

Miscellany 191:6-8
Miscellaneous Writings 172:16-17
Science and Health 242:15-20.

God is looking after Christian Science. Love protects all its ideas. God furnishes all thoughts to man. They think they can attack us mentally. They constantly suggest lust to Christian Scientists. They suggest it to their own laity. This belief seems to succeed sometimes, and you have to rebuke Roman Catholic influence. The claim of lust might be a belief of original sin.

Original Sin

Original sin is mortal mind in its worst form! It is of no importance that they curse. Have no fear of the curse. If a Protestant child is baptized by a nurse or relative, a claim has been established and must be broken. True baptism will take care of this.

The more debased will vehemently curse and try to imagine evil for an individual they would harm, or they will use the name of a person they would harm. They have images to malpractice on, and stick sharp instruments into it, to make the malpractice effective. Foot-podding is another claim to make people lame. The budding priests are all taught these things, and are taught to handle Christian Scientists in this way. They will sometimes center their thought and curse a single organ or every organ and work that way.

Treatment: There is no mental Inquisition; it is neither person, place nor thing. There is no malpractice at all.

Other religious bodies may be hostile to Christian Science, but they are not dangerous. They are not organized.

Manual of The Mother Church: Article 27: Section 4

We should not treat or teach anyone who has the slightest connection with the Roman Catholic church at the time of application. They must be free by the time they reach you. Always handle this thing with great love. The Roman Catholic church says once a Roman Catholic, always a Roman Catholic. We do not say it. A Roman Catholic can break away and become a Christian Scientist, but always enquire how the connection was broken. The connection is a mental one. Have they definitely broken their connection with the church? The church holds them with superstition and fear, and they are in terror of the priest.

Some who come out of Roman Catholicism are not very strong; and for their own protection, they should be well grounded before joining the church. While we should be careful, we should be just. It is always unjust to point out a person and say he is a former Roman Catholic.

Question: Why are Roman Catholic girls given as little education as possible and boys as much as possible?

Answer: That comes from an old error that believes that the male animal is naturally superior to the female.

When they come to you, ask about the baptism, consecrated ground, and so on; if they have belonged to a Protestant church, and how long since confession. It isn't enough for one to say he doesn't go to church or confession. Seemingly, Roman Catholicism is an aggressive and trained system of malpractice. The priests will try to follow them up even after they have joined the Christian Science church. Some terrible tragedies have occurred through Roman Catholicism and Christian Science marriages. Know that Roman Catholic baptism cannot hold them.

The Roman Catholic church would like nothing better than to have Christian Scientists fear them. It is nothing but a gigantic bluff wholly made up of fear and ignorance. The good in mortal mind is one of the worst things we have to deal with. The Roman Catholic good is far more vicious than its evil. You must know that Roman Catholicism cannot deceive the race through a belief of doing good, because what mortal mind calls good cannot deceive a Christian Scientist or anyone else.

Never give a position of trust to a Roman Catholic. They will work for years to gain your confidence, then will come a systematic betrayal which is part of the Roman Catholic training. Don't take a chance with any of them, as a Roman Catholic is always taught that the end justifies the means. Do not let your kindness of heart fool you. There can be no social relationship between Roman Catholics and Christian Scientists. A Roman Catholic situation will go along well until some condition will bring out a trick which no honorable person would do; it never fails. It is the Jesuit training. Wherever they can, they will discriminate against the Protestants and replace them with Catholics.

Science and Health 583:12-19

We cannot consider Roman Catholicism as a religion or a church, for it is neither one. It claims to be both for the purpose of deceiving the race. There is no truth or love in that organization and it certainly does not rest upon or proceed from divine Principle. It does not afford proof of its utility, and is not found elevating the race in any respect; nor is it found rousing the dormant understanding from material beliefs to the apprehension of spiritual ideas. That is the not the object of the Roman Catholic hierarchy. They have no intention of elevating the race; quite the reverse. This organization is dedicated to the purpose of tearing down and destroying everything good and everything that stands for Principle.

Roman Catholicism is not a church. It is a disease. Nor can it claim to be *the* church. It cannot deceive mankind into believing it is *the* church. It cannot make mankind believe that its institutions are any part of the structure of Truth and Love.

The ritualism, sophistry, dogmas and teachings of Roman Catholicism are not the word of God, but of Satan. Their teachings are not provable and have never been proved; and no Roman Catholic can prove them, for they are not demonstrable. They cannot heal, and they cannot save, and the laity are finding out that there is no salvation in Roman Catholicism or their so-called church. Basically, you could not have such a religion without a wicked God.

They say that their God knows evil and that He is infinite. If infinity knows evil, than you have got eternal, infinite wickedness, so you have got a wicked God in Roman Catholicism. Another thing, you must have a damned man in Roman Catholicism, or you can't have salvation in the church. You must have a wicked god and a damned man with a priest between them, and that constitutes the Roman Catholic church. Right at the start it has no power, for there is no power except infinity, and infinity is good.

The doctrines and institutions of Roman Catholicism spring from the worst passions, the most relentless lust, superstition, fear and gross materiality. The teachings of the Jesuit schools are characterized by spiritual ignorance, cruelty, tyranny, and the mercilessness of the dark ages. The so-called church is founded upon, and is the embodiment of dishonesty, deceit, craftiness, animal cunning, slander and every evil work. Their activities are characterized by scheming, intrigue and deceit. The hierarchy are thoroughly unprincipled men whose tools are human will, lust, hatred and dishonesty.

The claim is demonology, the deification of mind in matter. The only way to handle this evil is with great confidence and love, for no evil can stand in the presence of Love. The nature of Love is the extinguishment of evil. Roman Catholicism is today making frantic efforts to bolster up its tottering rottenness. The thing is disintegrating to its utter extinction and destruction. There are plenty of honorable men in that church who have never been touched by the ordinary low-down stuff that is taught in the Jesuit schools. They have never heard of it; but the great majority in this country, especially those educated in the Irish priesthood, are given this deceit.

Do not be disturbed by Roman Catholicism. You cannot be touched by it, if you do not believe in it. Our treatment against Roman Catholicism is not to hurt them, but to save every Roman Catholic on earth. We are not at war with anything but spiritual wickedness. Handle this claim every day. Make a point to educate yourself along this line, but don't be a specialist. Many Christian Scientists have made this claim very real by wrong work, and that is exactly what Roman Catholicism wants. You are not awake to this claim if you are afraid of it, or if you fail to handle it in a systematic manner.

Christian Scientists sometimes talk error instead of Truth, when they are taught that there is no error in Truth and no Truth in error. This claim is nothing to be afraid of, for there is no truth in it. Be calm and serene; sure in consciousness. They fear the calmness. In fact, if you lose your calmness, you lose your Science. Christian Science was established to break the claim that Roman Catholicism could darken human thought.

Roman Catholicism Handled

Know: Roman Catholicism cannot interfere with a Christian Science treatment any more than it can stop the sun from rising. Roman Catholicism has no entity or influence; no social, political, financial, educational, or philanthropical influence. Its claim of influence of any kind is broken forever through the revelation and demonstration of Christian Science.

It is a false claim, and it is not acting in belief or at all. It is not, cannot, and does not annul, interfere with, disturb, delay or reverse any declaration of Christian Science; nor can it in any way prevent or delay its full demonstration. It is without being, substance, truth, presence, activity, or manifestation, in God's creation. The Roman Catholic church is powerless, mindless, and lifeless. It does not belong to, nor is it any part of, anything that is true or infinite. It is negation, nothing; therefore anything that seems to be an influence in this belief, is neither thought nor influence.

Any effort that is made by way of prayer, curse, anathema, hypnotic effort, human will, or any other effort, is unknown to God; and man's realization that good alone is real, that good alone has power, presence and law, is a law of utter annulment and total extinction to the belief that Roman Catholicism could in any manner, through priests, relatives, friends or neighbors, interfere with the Christ, Truth, in human consciousness.

The mesmerism of Roman Catholicism is broken. It is nothing to be disturbed about. It cannot make men afraid to think. It cannot rob man of the power to recognize and hold fast to that which is good and true.

The spirit of Truth is come; the Science of Christianity is here. It is working in individual human consciousness, and is a spiritual law, a perpetual law of annihilation to every false claim opposed to the activity of good. Roman Catholicism cannot silence the eternal longing of the human heart to know God and be at peace. Their very effort to deny Christian Science and the activities of good, is a law of self-destruction to themselves. No mortal man can rule the earth in place of God; neither the Pope nor his hierarchy can prevent the laity from finding that out, for they can no longer be deceived.

Mortal Mind

It is tremendously important that we do no lose sight of the fact that the basic error is mortal mind. "The basic error is mortal mind." (*Science and Health*) Our work is to recognize and handle the claim of mortal mind, and make it powerless and impossible. Mortal mind is opposed by the Christ healing. Roman Catholicism and *materia medica* are not the only divisions of mortal mind that oppose the Truth.

Mortal mind is the error; and when there is a claim of mortal mind, it will oppose the Truth. We must recognize something about mortal mind that many do not recognize — *that is the whole of evil.* You might say that drink, lust, etc., are wrong; but the whole of mortal mind is wrong. A self-righteous and so-called good mortal is one of the worst phases of mortal mind. Mortal mind is not a fact; it is a false claim. It has its own concept of creation, and its belief is its false claim. *All* of its claims are false, a lie about the real. Mortal mind calls its projective beliefs matter, and the belief of matter is mortal mind.

This last statement will easily bear an hour's study. To analyze objects about us, we must see them as having less matter, or not any matter. When you let matter alone and handle claims wholly as claims of mortal mind so-called, you will have wonderful success in your work.

Mortal mind is simply a claim of mortality opposed to immortality, engaged wholly in murder and destruction. It is nothing but a belief, a lie about immortal Mind. *Error* is a word, and not the name of a thing. The words *mortal mind, animal magnetism,* and *error* always mean nothingness. A person uncovers error as something; but Truth uncovers error as nothing. In everything but Christian Science, we find the spirit of negation. Christian Science affirms.

Every claim of disease is a belief in mortal mind. It is not a condition of matter. If you treat disease, you make a mistake. There is no belief in mortal mind that cannot be corrected. Never doubt that you have the upper hand at all times. Through Christian Science, we have the ability and power to intelligently handle the belief of mental malpractice. Our work is to know the facts of Science so well that we can handle the claims of mortal mind with absolute confidence

Science and Health 419:16-19; 406:19-25

There are certain claims which mortal mind says are incurable, but they have all been healed in Christian Science. Doctors do not say there is an incurable disease; they say they do not know enough to cure them, that *materia medica* has not advanced enough to cure all diseases. The more advanced physicians say that the time will come when these diseases will be healed. They have that theory, and at least they believe that they might be cured when there is sufficient progress made in medical science.

Yet if they were suddenly to realize that all diseases are curable and could be cured without delay, they would be terrified and wonder what would become of them. Their hope is to keep the race sick, and it is not their fault either, for they have been educated that way. Don't blame them, for they didn't teach themselves what they know. They really do not want the race well, even though they say their object is to attain a science that will produce a healthy race.

Medical thought is based on negation. No matter what mortal mind says about disease being incurable, Christian Science can heal everything. Christian Science is the divine Christ made practical and available to every man, woman and child, here and now. It is revealed by God Himself, and is a constant revelation of infinite good, of Life and Love. It heals unfailingly, because treatment rests upon absolute fact.

There is no disease, and nobody has a disease. It is not Christian Science simply to say that everything is all right; that is not enough. Everything *is* all right, but you have to maintain that fact until things change. If you know God is all, you would heal every case with your first treatment. We know God *is* all; but you will have to bring your argument to the point where it will logically uphold your statement that God is all.

Error may find it possible to stand before a Christian Science practitioner and refuse to yield; but error cannot stand before God and refuse to yield. When you get yourself out of the way so that your treatment is nothing but the pure realization of God and His presence, error cannot stand and will not stand. The sooner you get the practitioner out of the way, the better. The claim is error versus Truth; and, of course, error does not exist. You cannot modify the meaning of the word *unreal*. There is never a moment when error could be real.

Mortal mind, or the human body, is a compound belief. It is called a material thing, but it is a belief, because Spirit could not make matter and matter could not make itself; and the only thing mortal mind has ever done, is to claim it has substance; and it calls that matter. Its belief of substance is disintegrating substance. Its size, weight, and other qualities are all beliefs; and they have no substance. The qualities of divine Mind are not material; and even size, weight, resistance, etc. are not real. Even adhesion, cohesion, and attraction, as Mrs. Eddy says, are properties of Mind and not of matter.

There is one Mind. The claim that there is another mind, mortal and limited, is but a lie without any principle, substance, or law. It is untrue and impossible. The claim that there is mortality, or malicious mentality, is a false claim. That a thought of mortality or malice can be transferred by any known or unknown means, is a false claim. There is no such power as thought transference, no thought waves, no thought vibrations, no thought circles. Thought has its being in God; and if a person has any thoughts at all, they come from God; consequently the claim of malpractice is a lie; it has no substance, soul, intelligence, or presence, and is a false claim.

Metaphysically considered, what we have to meet is nothing. And nothing can do nothing at any time, at any place, to anyone; and the practice of nothingness — which is all there is to mental malpractice — can accomplish nothing.

There is one Mind. The claim that there is another mind, mortal and limited, is but a lie without any principle, substance, or law. It is untrue and impossible. The claim that there is mortality, or malicious mentality, is a false claim. That a thought of mortality or malice can be transferred by any known or unknown means, is a false claim. There is no such power as thought transference, no thought waves, no thought vibrations, no thought circles. Thought has its being in God; and if a person has any thoughts at all, they come from God; consequently the claim of malpractice is a lie; it has no substance, soul, intelligence, or presence, and is a false claim.

Metaphysically considered, what we have to meet is nothing. And nothing can no nothing at any time, at any place, to anyone; and the practice of nothingness — which is all there is to mental malpractice — can accomplish nothing.

Maternity

The *Manual*, page 88, Article 18, Section 1, Board of Education states: "Obstetrics will not be taught." Obstetrics cannot be taught. We do not teach obstetrics.

Always work under the law of the State. Have help from some doctor or nurse who has had experience with cases and is informed about the claims associated with the case. Man's spiritual being, being one with God, can never make anyone suffer, never had any period of gestation, never came out of anything, but is forever free from objectionable features before or ever after.

Man is never born; he is always a spiritual, perfect idea, forever the manifestation or expression of the divine Mind, or true appearance and harmonious action, and the unfoldment of true ideas. True ideas are always properly and perfectly presented.

Declare the truth that God and man are one. This is a protection for mother and child. Handle this claim diligently. Handle fear. Love alone is present. Handle the belief of pain by knowing that real creation is harmonious and perfect. Know the pre-existence of child as well as mother. Realize the truth about real substance. The belief in the case is that the mother might be injured. Realize the truth about body. Man is the body of God, and not material.

Matter is subservient to Spirit. Spiritual understanding controls matter. Handle obstruction as it relates to man and body. Nothing obstructs the truth and Truth alone is real.

Afterbirth

Science and Health 463: 12-13. Note marginal heading "Scientific Obstetrics." "A spiritual idea has not a single element of error, and this truth removes properly whatever is offensive." A true idea can do no harm at any time. Realize the truth about individual man, perfect individuality now and immediately after birth. Don't feel rushed about the case. Always protect your patients against outsiders talking about the claims.

Every Treatment

Question: What should be in every treatment?
Answer: *Cause, law, substance.*

Sight

No disease, injury, or blindness, has ever touched eyes. There is not any disease or weakness to touch them. The facilities of the divine Mind can never be lost or injured or impaired. Sight is Mind. The only Mind there is, is right here; and that is perfect sight. We need to claim it now, and continue to claim it forever. We can now begin to see with the divine Mind.

All is infinite consciousness. There is one eye and one sight. It is Mind. It is mine. We need to change our seeing, and not the thing seen. Sight becomes clearer when we understand that the things seen and the seer are one. The thing that sees and the thing seen are one. The thing reading and thing being read are one — one consciousness.

It might be that your work would lead the patient to demonstrate a correct pair of glasses. It might be that he would have to demonstrate the glasses first as a step, if he has to. If you hate glasses, you would not get any place; you will not get rid of them that way. Of course, glasses are really an obstruction, a belief that we need a little more matter to see with. The belief of glasses is no worse than the belief of material eyesight. Sight is consciousness, or a conscious function of Mind. There is no sense in matter; sense is spiritual. Mind never ceases to see.

Mind sees, so the sight of Mind is manifested. Sight is the eternal mandate of Mind. We read and see with Mind. Use your sight, not your eyes. We have one kind of sight, one kind of eye — spiritual.   Let eyes and sight be one — that one is sight. We all have one sight.

There is no destructive element in sight, the sight of Mind. I have eternal, perfect sight because God gave it to me, and nothing can take it away. Seeing and hearing are purely mental. All we have to do is to know it.

The belief of advancing years should always be taken into consideration. Sight is unchangeable. Sight is indestructible. Time is but a period of progress, and sight must improve. It is the business of eyes to see, and they will do so forever. The belief of eyes is the effort of mortal eyes to see. Immortal Mind is true sight, perfect sight, eternal sight. You can't separate sight from eye. All is Mind. Every faculty is perfect.

Everything that is to be seen is Mind. It is all here. That which is seeing is Mind. Mind cannot see anything that is outside of consciousness. Sight is Mind, and Mind is sight. Sight for the divine man is natural and always perfect. Nothing can impair that sight. Nothing can make it deteriorate. No belief of age can touch it; no claim of accident can touch it; no medical theory can encroach upon its beauty, for in God there is no such belief. Man looking through Soul sees nothing but beauty and perfection. There is but one eye, and that is beauty and perfection. Sight is spiritual perception. God is the absolute power that prevents deterioration of the belief of sight. The law of Mind is entire restoration to the belief of impaired vision.

Hearing

Mind is hearing. The divine idea has to be humanly expressed. You have to bring the spiritual fact to human consciousness. It is not possible that man can lose his hearing, or have it interfered with; nor can it be subject to any other law than that of perfect continuity. All his functions are eternal and perfect as God.

Nothing can ever interfere with his hearing; it is always sustained. His hearing can never deteriorate. His hearing can never become obscure. His hearing now exists in perfection; and it is the law of God that he shall hear forever as God hears; and this law is in this treatment made effective and operative.

It is the presence of God and the power of God that is operating in this treatment, and acting as this treatment. This power or law of God which is operating as this treatment, which is God, is omnipotence, and the law to annul any belief of impaired hearing or deafness. It is a law of annulment to anything that claims to be a cause of impaired hearing. It destroys all so-called laws associated with the claim.

Hearing is a spiritual sense, is Mind hearing. Hearing is Mind. Like sight, the thing that we hear with and the thing that we hear are one Mind. Hearing is a function of Mind, and you will have to see that no function, or activity, of the divine Mind can ever be impaired. If you are clear about this, you would establish hearing for a person who had his eardrums pierced. You can absolutely restore the function irrespective of the organ, if you understand that the faculty of function is a spiritual activity. Sometimes a person tends to show it in the voice. The claim is in the throat in many instances. Again, it might be the claim of the hardening of the eustachian tube which does not permit the normal flow of secretion. The fact is, he is not deaf. You cannot repair his hearing any more than you can repair God. There is only one hearing and nothing ever happened to that.

Cancer — Tumor — Growth

It is claimed that cancer, tumors, and growths are incurable. Always bear in mind that these are only names — not names of diseases, but names of beliefs.

Moreover, the claim cannot be designated by name, because the fear is deeper in human consciousness than the name of this disease; therefore metaphysical healing is the only thing that holds any hope, since it gets at the claim fundamentally by getting rid of the beliefs which constitute it.

In handling these claims, it is not necessary to probe the consciousness of the patient; that is an improper thing to do. It is rather so clarifying his thought that pure spiritualization reveals and destroys the underlying belief.

It is not necessarily the patient's thought entirely; it may be, and often is, that he is imposed upon by heredity beliefs, and in other ways. We do not always get at the root of things by assuming that the patient is more than a victim; and if we think he is a criminal, or if we think that he is really to blame for his own thought, we are off the track. We should never lose sight of the fact that the basic error is mortal mind, and that he is a victim, rather than a criminal.

Make a distinct denial of mental malpractice, because the patient has been subjected to medical examination, and somebody has said that he could not get well. That always needs specific denial. Always know that matter or evil has no place, time, position, power or law. There is no incurable disease.

What constitutes the difference between what are called incurable diseases and curable diseases? Less fear of the curable disease. In Science, what is the reason that every disease is curable? Because Christian Science is equal to every demand, to every need, to every occasion, to every event. *There is no incurable disease.*

All disease is a belief in mortal mind, and not for an instant is it outside of what is called mortal mind. It is never in the body or on the body. It is not in matter; it is only a belief. Never treat matter. "When we remove disease by addressing the disturbed mind, giving no heed to the body, we prove that thought alone creates the suffering." (Science *and Health* 400:20-22)

When there is cancer to be considered, always know that your treatment reaches the very depths of mortal belief with its healing light. In these cases, you will find hidden away there such claims as sorrow, grief, intense self-pity, sadness, disappointment, regret, unsatisfied longings, intense desire, or something along that line.   It might be any of them, some of them, or all of them. The patient might be habitually bitter, depressed, or overwhelmed with a dismal fear. Always handle a vindictiveness when the claim is malignant. Make yourself clear on this point. The emotions do not produce the claim: they *are* the claim.

There is no belief of mortal mind that is incapable of being corrected. It is inevitably true that you can correct any error, if you know enough; and Christian Science is the Science by which you know enough to correct any error; and it will not make a particle of difference whether the error said it was an incurable disease, or a headache, or anything else.

There is no incurable disease. You know it intellectually, but you must know it practically. Don't believe it. *Know it.* A cold and a cancer are on the same plane, and one is no more real than the other. You will have to know that the mental image of the disease cannot affect your treatment. If the doctor has left because he thinks the case hopeless, handle the belief that he thinks it is incurable, and that mortal mind thinks the same. You know that this is only a state of mortal mind and ignorance. The claim may be only a seeming penalty for having been sorrowful and bitter.

Fear is all there is to the claim of incurableness. Handle fear thoroughly, and know that there is nothing in consciousness that can take on darkness or fear. The material body is a state of fear. The real body and consciousness can never be touched by such a thing; and in the whole realm of Truth, there is no such thing as a cancer. Mind is the only body there is, and this treatment is the law of expulsion to the belief of cancer, the exclusion and the annulment of it.

Know that your treatment is the activity of the divine Christ, the invincible law of Love and harmony flooding consciousness with light and love, to the complete removal of fear, bitterness, sorrow and disease. These beliefs are like mushrooms that grow in cellars which are damp, dismal and depressing. Get rid of the cellar. Let in the light, and the mesmerism will lift. It is always good to know what substance is in these cases.

Tuberculosis

Tuberculosis is a belief that substance can disintegrate. Establish substance as the basic fact, and then deny the false claim. You restore substance because you have a realization of the real body. Do not let your patient say he has no body. Get him to declare the allness of God and man, the perfection of body. Disease is a specific error about body; consequently a specific statement of Truth is necessary to correct it. The specific error about the body is that it is a limited dimensional form of material elements, consisting of organs and functions.

The specific corrective idea about body is that the true body is a divine, infinite idea composed of Spirit, imperishable substance consisting of divine ideas forever eternal and active. God is perfect substance, and man is the image and likeness of this substance. His body is therefore tangible and always existing. The claim is mostly fear. He has a mental reservation that no matter what is done for him, he will not get well. Handle mesmerism.

When people say they are getting better, and they seem to be getting sweet, you will have to do very good work. It is a claim that they are getting a false sense of spiritual things, and are just fading out. Know that your treatment takes care of that error. Harmony is as eternal as God, and we are not depending upon the evidence of the senses.

The substance of lungs is Mind, perfect and infinite. They belong to creation, and cannot be destroyed. The evidence of God does not fade out any more that God fades out. We are not asked to do anything more than know. Christian Science does not ask *you* to heal the sick; it says "know the truth" and God will heal the sick.

Know that the spiritual body is so substantial, so tangible, so real, that true spirituality is a practical thing. For destroyed tissues, make the declaration that they are restored by Christian Science treatment, because substance has never been destroyed. God is primarily substance. In that substance there is no pain, no incurable disease, no disintegration, no weakness, no loss. In that substance there is only presence, and this is substance itself, strength, harmony, continuity and joy, and without disease.

There is no substance out of which matter could be made. The claim is a substanceless lie without cause, foundation, Principle, activity, or manifestation. There is no substance out of which it could be made. It is without space, place, occupancy, entity, or expression. It is the shadow of an impossible lie, without existence.

Sin

It is Christian Science practice to forgive sin by seeing the unreality of it. Establish the fact that there is no sin. Understanding is the Saviour. The tendency is to bind one with the shackles of false belief.

It is not the business of the Christian Scientist to say, "Well, he has sinned, now he will have to suffer it out." God never arranged such a thing for a sinner. God has only arranged for his redemption. There is no punishment for sin; forgiveness is the cure. The belief that one has to suffer for sin, is mortal mind, a false belief. God has no thought of sin, so man cannot have; therefore man is sinless. Sin is the basic error that mortal mind is a creator, consisting of different bodies involved in a sense of error. The basic error is fear, and Christ is the remedy for everything.

There is nothing to punish with; no one to punish man; and no one to be punished. God's law has no penalty. God's law means redemption without penalty. Know that man cannot be condemned. Condemn the sin, but not the sinner. Rebuke the error, but always with Truth.

How could you go to a case which appears to be the result of sin, and heal that case which appeared to be the result of sin, unless you knew enough to rebuke the belief of sin with its own nothingness? The mortal mind's sense of it is that the penalty follows the sin, and that it is bound to follow sin in all its various phases.

According to mortal mind the greatest sins do not carry with them a penalty. The greatest sins are the ones that Jesus condemned — hatred, malice, revenge, fear, backbiting and gossip. These are the greatest sins; and people do not think that there is any particular penalty following these; and yet they are more to be condemned than the sins that are incidental to a false sense of life and living. The nature of mortal mind is injustice and vengeance.

This belief of penalty must be wiped out completely. It tries to keep a person in hell for years after he has forgotten the sin. The sin might not have been anything very much, but the penalty very great. He fears the penalty more than the sin, and he is just as much afraid when he says, "I am good." In fact, he is more afraid of the punishment then. We will have to change this.

Christian Science would not be of any value to the world if it did not do something for these people, because mortal mind has done nothing but condemn and damn them to hell. Christian Science comes to save that which was lost; and we cannot possibly do it if we think man is a sinner, that he ever sinned, or could sin.

Penalty is always in mortal mind, and you must handle it as a claim and see its nothingness. It is not according to God that there is a penalty for some wrong act. Perhaps the act is not nearly as wrong as some other act that had no penalty. Man never was a sinner, and that is the reason he can be saved. If he had been a sinner, he would be one forever. Handle the belief of penalty, fear, ignorance and sin, but begin with penalty. Go right after the penalty, for that is where error claims to operate.

Science and Health says God does not punish anything but sin. That is to be explained by this: When Truth begins to appear in thought, very often its activity seems to be a sort of punishment. There is a kind of regret that there had ever been anything unlike Truth in our thought. If you let that in, and let it get hold of you, there will be a kind of penalty. Christian Science takes away all of that, and gives us the assurance that belongs to our divine nature, and establishes it firmly. Sin is unreal, is not a cause, and can have no effect or penalty. There is absolutely no penalty for anything you ever did or never did. Know that belief of penalty cannot do anything. There will never be any salvation so long as there is a belief of penalty.

Christian Science is a moral science, and will have to be carried on by strong men and women. Practitioners should stand for and inculcate the highest morality. They must shun even the appearance of evil. Not one of us can put himself on a very high pedestal; but get away from the worst to the better, and you will find your thinking accomplishing results.

Science and Health 192:17-21; 366:3-10

The so-called good person might be, and probably is, much more material than a bad one. The materiality of a self-righteous person is more difficult to heal than the materiality of the so-called sinner. Righteousness is never self-righteousness.

There is a distinction between sin and vice. All materiality, whether good or bad, is sin. The incidents that make a sinner are no worse than the belief of separation of God and man, or the belief that man is material.

It is necessary for everybody to work along this line to heal himself: I never committed any sins, never was a sinner; the whole thing is a dream; it never happened, even in belief. There never was a first sin, or a first sinner. I was never born a sinner, never manifested sin, never heard of sin, do not know it now, and never can know it; sin does not exist in the divine Mind, or in the divine idea; and I have nothing to do with it; and it has nothing to do with me. The division of beliefs — here is good and here is sin, evil — is nothing but mortal mind.

Science and Health 213:11-12; 327:31-2

Our government has to punish crime. It has to punish in the only way criminals understand; but when a person comes to you for help in Christian Science, lift him up. "Neither do I condemn thee. Go and sin no more."

It is futile and foolish to suppose that any person can hope to destroy the ills of the flesh while gratifying what appears to be even harmless appetites. Sometimes one cannot understand at first why he should give up smoking, and yet the hold smoking has upon him is the strongest possible reason why he should gain his freedom from this appetite. This also applies to other appetites.

The sooner people learn to eliminate the sensual elements from anything, the better their chances of demonstrating Christian Science and the unreality of matter. When the belief of pleasure in matter is destroyed, nothing remains to express desire, regardless of the hold material things may have upon the affections. "Higher enjoyments alone can satisfy the cravings of immortal man." We must give up all else to make room for spiritual growth.

Everyone knows that it is the belief of pleasure in matter, and not of pain in matter, that obstructs the world in its effort to free itself. We are alert to deny the least indication of physical discord, but to make our demonstration complete we should be just as alert to prove the nothingness of pleasure in the body.

Our sensuous appetites must be wiped out, whether they appear gross or refined, damaging or harmless. None are harmless. Each one carries the seed of destruction. The persistent effort to destroy the belief of pleasure in matter has its reward in the increased ability to destroy the sense of pain in matter.

There is no law of necessity that can force anyone to pick up evil suggestions and make them part of one's thinking. On the contrary, it is man's privilege and right to think in accordance with the divine Mind, and thus elude all of the pitfalls prepared by the cunning of the carnal mind.

When we wake up, we find that all of our enemies are but dead things, lifeless, because they are not of God. All of the suggestions that seem to surround us are dead, and they never did live. Our fear and indolence gave them a spurious life and activity which is destroyed by Christian Science.

Nerves

What seems to be a nervous system, is only mortal mind acting as its own influence on its belief of body. The belief about the human mind is that it exists in the head, and that it communicates itself by means of the nervous system to other parts of the human frame. Nerves claim to be a sort of telegraphic system, having a head central office and a number of substations, nerve-centers, all over the body, connected by a system of nerves: in other words, a claim of separation.

The claim is that the brain is the seat of intelligence, and radiating therefrom we have two sets of things called nerves. One set conveys the word, or desire, to various parts of the body, the other set brings back the message that the thing is done. It is a prevalent belief that many diseases result from the crossing of the two sets — that one nerve or set of nerves interferes with another set. That is the osteopathic belief, and should be handled as a claim by knowing God's ideas cannot interfere with one another.

The system of telepathy is a false claim because the divine Mind is never objective to His expression. God is not working *through* things; He is All-in-all. The divine Mind does not know anything separate from itself. Its infinite creation is itself.

According to belief the nervous system is the chief thing about a human being. The claim of nerves is one of the modern claims. The nervous system isn't any more real than sleep, and it hasn't any more substance than sleep. Sleep is a belief that there is something different from consciousness, that there is something different from unity. The divine Mind and divine idea are unity; they are poised together in strength and harmony.

In some way, we need to get rid of the belief that we are dependent upon a nervous system, because we are not. We are dependent upon Mind. When you recognize the divine fact that you and your Father-Mother Mind, cannot be separated, that every organ and function of the infinite embodiment of Being is saying I AM, then you will see what your real nerve is; and you will find a perfect nervous system in belief.

The nervous system spiritually understood, means simply the omnipresence of the divine Mind, always expressing itself to its own idea immediately, so that every idea has the Father-Mother Mind as its source, substance, and direction.

There is nothing true about the transmission of ideas except that they are never transmitted. Everything that constitutes you or me, is governed directly by the divine Mind. The claim is that you have distance between God and idea; the fact is, there is only unity of being; there is the immediate presence of Mind in every idea. Its every action is but the action of Mind saying I AM. The idea is glorifying God because it is God. It knows no separation from God.

The only nerve, therefore, is the fact of the inseparability of God and man, Mind and idea. The Truth about nerve is the presence of God. Everything it does is based on that belief.

A good nervous system is absolutely essential to a healthy person. We can have it the moment we realize that we are not dependent upon it. The day that a nervous person takes his stand that there is but one Mind, he will stop being nervous.

Power and control are immediate and not transmitted. Know that idea is controlled immediately as presence, and there are no nerves in Mind, and that there are no nerves in matter. Handle the belief that man exists apart from God.

A Word about Oneness

God and man are one. God and man are the same, but not the same one; man is one with God, but God is the infinity of man, and man is an infinite idea. God is infinity; man is not infinity. Man is infinite, but he is not infinity. Man expresses God, but not all of God. You cannot know the whole of God, but you can know the wholeness of God. You cannot be greater than God. We express the allness, but not the all, of God.

Infinity is God, and God is infinity. Man is infinite, one with infinity. Infinity is Principle. Infinity is a word with just one meaning, self-existent entity, the one divine Principle, Mind, Spirit, Soul, the first great cause and creator, God. That is infinity. Man is the expression of infinity, not separated from infinity. The expression is never separated from its Principle, and divine relationship never gets out of order. It is perfect forever.

Eczema

Always handle the belief of nerves with this claim. Handle irritability also. Doctors claim it is a condition of the blood, but they don't know much about it. It is not considered dangerous. Some forms of it are syphilitic; then it is a different thing. Then it is not eczema, although it appears very much like it.

It appears to be visible; but in Christian Science treatment, the whole thing is seen as mesmerism. You have to know that the people who see it cannot add to it, that the general mesmeric belief who sees it cannot operate.

Know that your treatment is a law of isolation to the case. Know that no human thought, or belief, can in any way assert itself, or express itself, or operate as law. Know that there is no pity, sympathy, or anything else, to augment the claim. Handle disappointment, regret, fear, and things of that kind. Be wary, and handle rebelliousness, bitterness, some sense of self that is hurt, suppressed, and unhappy.

General Practice

Science and Health 416:24-2; 417:27-4; 447:16-20
Miscellaneous Writings 358:4-8
Rudimental Divine Science 15:16-18
Science and Health 444:7-12; 452:18-27;
    445:8-18; 495:14; 464:13-19

The practitioner should be very wise. Don't explain too much. The practitioner should always be confident and patient. The patient does not have to confess to the practitioner. Truth will do the probing. Don't be curious about your patients.

Make the whole thing sacred. If you are not watchful, you will hear so many things unlike God that it will be a cross to you;

and you don't want to carry any crosses. That doesn't mean that you are to ignore the error; but mortals must learn that by contemplating, rehearsing, and reporting evil, they are magnifying their belief in it.

To hold evil in thought long enough to express it audibly to another, is a great mistake. There is no doubt that if those who talk evil would wait until they had destroyed all sense of its reality in their own thought before speaking of it, all of the evil speaking would be done away with. If you are wrong, don't argue. If you are right, why argue?

We must practice persistently, scientifically, practically, and unfailingly. A Christian Scientist must not shirk anything. If you shirk anything, you have fear; and if you have fear, you lack love; and if you lack love, you are not a Christian Scientist. Go on working for any claim.

Luke 11:5-8; 18:1-5
Science and Health 400:18-19; 261:4-7; 418:5-6

Beware of believing that specific sins must be uncovered before your patient can be healed. Individual faults might produce the disorder, but this is not always the case. In mortal mind, the cause cannot always be traced, simply because the belief may be in mortal law.

Science and Health 419:1-4

Physical disorder is always the result of error of some kind, but sometimes it is only something the patient has accepted. To uncover error means to uncover it to ourselves and not always to the patient.

Truth and Love uncover error to see its nothingness. Beware of *rebuking*. The best rebuking of error is to heal the case. Patients may not have had any desire to sin, but were handled by animal magnetism. If you seek a fault, seek it with the light of Truth and Love.

Don't say, "Get over your resentment." Know he hasn't any resentment. Demonstrate the real practice. Whatever the claim is, handle it; don't make something of it. If a person is angry, don't tell him he must get over his anger before he can get over his disease. His disease *is* his anger; that is the matter with him.

Sometimes the easiest person to heal is the one who has the least idea that he is good, or that he wants to be good. You cannot put it on the basis of what is ordinarily called righteousness, for the simple reason that sometimes people who are righteous are only inexperienced — that's all.

They have been going along through the world very much protected, and they have some beliefs, and these beliefs are said to be good. They are good because they haven't been tempted. Very often a person has gone through a perfect hell of temptation, and perhaps knows enough of hell not to be even curious about knowing more of it. A great many people who sin, sin through curiosity. The vice of the world goes on solely because of that. It is just mortal mind's desire to know; and, of course, Christian Science handles that.

Put it on the basis of whether the patient is ready or not. This is something hard to determine; the Christ alone can reveal it through your consecration to your work, and your knowing that there is nothing appearing as part of the day's activities that is not sent of God. Wisdom as to what courses to take, will come as part of your demonstration. In your practice, turn your patient toward God; the practitioner should talk less and know more.

Let the patient unload and relieve his mind; listen and reverse the error. No matter what the claim is, seek the counter-fact. Let your patient get it out all at once; if you do not let him talk, you will not know what to reverse. Be a good listener and know the Truth. Never introduce your patients, or make a show of your practice.

If you are called out on a case, don't hurry. Your work and attitude must always be peaceful and calm. When you go in the strength of the Lord (understanding), you know that no one is ill; that man is perfect, whole and complete; that no mortal law is operating on his body; that Christian Science is the only law working on his body — that is, the law of God. Before you start, get the kingdom of God and keep it holy. Existence apart from God is error; and if we acknowledge that anyone is ill, discouraged or sinful, we are in error as much as they are.

The claim of mental malpractice is that it can build up in the thought of the practitioner mental images; and when that occurs, one has the impression he is treating a disease, and that it is something that can be seen and felt. It is nothing but the suggestion of malpractice, and should be handled as such so that no image of disease occupies the thought. If, in spite of yourself, the image persists, then declare that notwithstanding this malpractice, the Christ heals the disease, and you will be free from that claim.

Live your own life, and don't let anyone think for you. Do your own thinking. Be yourself. When a practitioner is working rightly, he is not limiting himself. The mental attitude that is like omniscience, is the only correct attitude to produce correct results, and make our practice in the highest degree successful. He need not be afraid that by glorifying his treatment he is glorifying himself. Manifestly, if he is thinking of himself, he is not giving a treatment. Inspiration is important, but we need to be well grounded in the letter. You will not be easily handled if you are able to go through the process of treatment in detail, to the letter. The one who can give a clear treatment without any holes in it, is the one you can count on. Of course, it is not what you repeat, but what you *know* that counts.

Your treatment is one with God, and operates according to Mind's power and presence. The power of Christian Science treatment knows no restrictions; its power is infinite and omnipotent to establish harmony wherever it seems to be absent. The absence of good and Truth is obviously impossible to one who knows the nature of Mind. Exalt your Science and not yourself. Divine Science humanly demonstrated will give you good, sound human judgment.

Hypnotism is practiced by members of the medical profession; and naturally they are inclined to use it against anything they fear; and the claim is that they do fear the power of Christian Science to heal the sick.

All that is needed in the world is Love: not merely loving, which is wonderful, but Love itself. If you really love a person, see him as never material. The nothingness of materiality in Love, is the only real way to handle anything.

The practitioner is not a channel; he is the presence and activity of divine Science. The presence of God is what heals, and the more the practitioner sees this the better. The general statements as to the fact that God governs the universe, are not more effectual in helping a given circumstance than they would be before you made them, unless you made them effectual.

The evidence of the treatment is the conscious knowledge on the part of the practitioner that something is going on in the case because of what he is knowing. Something in the way of God's power and presence, is being demonstrated because of what the practitioner knows. The statements of Science are tremendously helpful, and people get a great deal out of them and all that; but they don't always serve as a treatment unless you know it is a treatment. Many a practitioner has failed in his work because he was not sure of himself; he believed, but he didn't know. *You must know, and know that you know.*

Never take a case with the attitude that you will do the best you can; that is not a fair proposition for the patient. When you take a case, you take it to heal. Know that you reflect and express divine power and are an absolute law to the case; and thus you get the practitioner out of the way.

There are four things in a treatment: God or Truth, man, practitioner, and error. Get the practitioner out of the way; let Truth destroy the error.

Do not erect in imagination a sick person or a well one, and try to heal him mentally. You do not hold a person in thought at all; you are handling cases, not people. The belief will always yield to the fact. Never name a disease to the patient. Do not talk too long to your patients; not over fifteen minutes of straight Science, for that is about all they can take unless they are well grounded.

The practitioner should be well and keep well. The hard work in practice is a mistake; the sense of being burdened is a false sense and is wrong. The practice should be joyful as we go along. No matter how large one's practice, he should be perfectly free; because if we become burdened, our work begins to be less than scientific. If there is ever a time when there is no joy in your work, you are not in a position to do the work.

There is no need of two practitioners on a case; there should be only one at a time. Some cases malpractice on themselves in their eagerness to get a healing. Seek good and favorable conditions for your patients. In corresponding with patients, nothing of a confidential nature should be dictated to a secretary. Be wise in making inquiries about patients after treatment; you might start something. Don't overload with patients; let them go to someone else.

A good test of a treatment is to work until you are perfectly calm.

Watch your phone conversations, but don't be afraid.

Elimination

Our so-called body, a compound belief, includes within itself this necessity in order to be a good one and a normal one, which has to be fed. In order to be healthy, it has to have what is called digestion, assimulation, and nutrition.

Not all of the food that goes into the human frame is nutritive. Some of it is eliminated because it is of no value so far as nutrition is concerned. The action of Truth on behalf of the human body, understood properly (when a person realizes he hasn't a material body, but that body is infinite and spiritual, and when realization is so clear that there is no doubt about it), that understanding on behalf of the human body will eliminate the waste properly and entirely, and will leave the body free from any wrong effect which occurs when waste is retained.

If thought is quite clear regarding man's spiritual being, so that the human body is forgotten in the realization of the omnipotence and omni-action of God, then the human body will experience that very thing; and that which doesn't belong to it, which is not healthy for it, is eliminated by the very power and presence of that law. That will be your work, to a very large extent, for we are not where we can ignore the belief that it is better to have normal functions and normal elimination.

If you can see there is no elimination in Truth; that Truth is infinite; that infinite Principle is self-operation, omniscient in the universe of infinite spiritual action, fills all space, and there is nothing else going on, you would have perfect elimination; for Truth, there is never an insufficient action, nor any disturbed action that is lost or inoperative. If there is a lack of elimination, you establish good elimination by finding out there is no elimination in infinity.

The law of God as presence, is an absolute law of removal to the belief of retention of poisonous substance in the body or on the body.

There is no accumulation in the divine Mind; there is nothing in the universe that is not active. If anything exists, it exists according to activity. Now, elimination has to happen; and there is but one way to handle it; and you will always handle it if you see it right, and that is the way of infinity. That doesn't mean there is such a thing as infinite elimination, for elimination has nothing to do with infinity; but infinite realization will demonstrate perfect elimination. There is no elimination in infinity, and yet in a human body there is constant elimination. The claim does not exist in the organ; it is in mortal mind. You don't have to handle the material body; you handle the human belief.

Defective elimination, in belief, causes many diseases. In belief, it is said to cause rheumatism, swollen joints, and even mortality. In a case of tonsillitis, always handle it; also in a tubercular claim; and in a case of enlarged glands, etc. The beliefs that are wrong, are the only things to be eliminated.

There is also the belief that the elimination of cellular tissue stops, and that produces old age. The organs of elimination are the lungs, bowels, liver, kidneys, and pores; and all of these ideas are really spiritual; therefore they are always perfect, harmonious, active, and sustained by spiritual law.

There should be sufficient bodily activity. Even Christian Scientists cannot get along without a correct amount of activity; and if they are wise, they won't try. Be active. It is just as much a part of God's plan that you can walk and move and have your being in an active physical way as that you can think the Truth, and it is just as much a part of that purpose that this action should be demonstrated.

What we call body is a substratum of mortal mind, and a condi-tion that demands two phases of activity — intake and outgo. To handle the belief of obstruction by dead matter, see that the infinity of being is not intake and outgo, that man is ceaseless receptivity and reflection.

In the divine order of being, there isn't a thing to eliminate; and if you are clear about that, your treatment becomes a law to the belief of defective elimination, and establishes complete, thorough and harmonious elimination.

Law

All laws are laws of Spirit; and the perversion of them gives us what are called laws of nature; and they result in sin, sickness and death of the human race. All sickness is according to false belief; all the people that suffer, sin, and die, do so through the belief of the activity and operation of false laws. In absolute Truth,

God never made any laws. The Mind which is too pure to behold iniquity, knows nothing unlike itself to make corrective laws for.

In the highest sense, there are no material laws, for law is mental. In the divine order of Science, the divine law is the law of harmony, health and security to man as the creation of divine Principle. The law of God wipes out any other law. The law of God is a law of completeness and continuity. The divine law in your treatment is total annulment to the so-called laws of false belief.

A person must first be obedient to moral laws, so that he will see and obey and understand spiritual law. *All that you need to know, can be known in an instant.* We must do better and progress higher everyday. The law of God is tangible and indestructible. *Put that in every treatment. Let your treatment know enough to know of itself as law.*

Law is the mandate of Mind, the first great cause. It is God acting in His own creation. The practitioner is advocate, judge, jury, and law — all of them. Your decision is the decision in the case. You control the situation.

There is no material law, because matter cannot think to make laws. It is not that you know the law; *you are law to the case.* It never happened when you say it didn't, when you say it and know it. You are the law to the case, or else you had better not be on the case. The nature of law is omni-action, its substance is Mind, and its enforcement is Truth.

Poise

The divine Mind and the divine idea are poised together in strength and harmony. The divine will of Mind is the divine action of the idea.

More about Treatment

There are two phases of practice we need to watch out for and avoid. One is to be over-anxious; that attitude will interfere with your work. The other is to become so accustomed to the work of Science that you become stale. There is nothing going on unless you are progressing; and if you fall into either of these habits, you are in a bad way. If a person knew enough, he could give a much better treatment without argument.

Words are nothing in this work; *knowing is everything.* When the divine Mind talks and announces its own power and presence; when the divine Christ comes to the flesh to destroy incarnate error; when Truth is seen to be the only presence, the only power and law; when God is seen to be all, then argument is not necessary. The argument is really self-treatment to get yourself to the point of realization for both practitioner and patient. If you meet the case with divine Love, that is the real and ultimate need, the ultimate method.

You must be able to handle claims in detail; but on the other hand, if you were handling a case and there came to you a clear realization of the infinite presence of God and the perfection of man, and your understanding was so clear that you didn't have even a sense of a patient, but only a clear sense of unity and sonship with infinite Mind, you would have nothing to do but stand and calmly know. This is the pure, scientific way, and the correct practice of the other ways will strengthen us in attaining the scientific way.

When these claims are uncovered, they are two-thirds destroyed, and the other one-third destroys itself; but let your treatment be so clear that when an error is uncovered, it is *all* destroyed, for the claim has been uncovered, not as something, but as nothing.

If something has been uncovered, never let your patient condemn himself; you can never heal through condemnation. The way to forget and heal it, is to make nothing of it, and to do it so thoroughly that it will never appear again in belief. Make it a rule in your life to always look into consciousness with Science. Do not look into it with condemnation.

You must have respect for what you know, and for the treatment which expresses your knowledge of Christian Science. You have to have certain reverence for it; it is a sacred thing; it is divine; it is God's treatment; you cannot put limitation on it after it is given, by thinking it is your treatment. Glorify God's treatment and forget yourself, otherwise you will crucify the Christ in you, and that is mortal mind's desire. Let your thoughts assume the power and majesty of the divine Mind. Your treatment is not the Truth about God; it is the Truth which *is* God.

Good intentions are animal magnetism, because they always imply weak action. You will hear Christian Scientists say, "I will do it, if it is right," when they should say, "I will do it because right *is*."

There is no set form for a treatment, and no one can give a form, simply because the growing understanding of Christian Science constitutes the real treatment to the case and determines its efficacy. Treatment does not consist of statements; the object is *realization*.

Unless you are alert and watchful, much of the wording of a treatment is likely to become somewhat conventional, and I will ask you to avoid that. There are two things to watch out for; there is the person who works along certain definite lines, and is very careful to give a treatment in great detail, handling everything thoroughly in every treatment. He is liable to become somewhat tied up with his own method; he is so conscientious that he becomes involved in a labored treatment. On the other hand, there is the person who has no method at all; his treatment is indistinct, doesn't handle the claim, doesn't even fit the case; his treatment is so indefinite that it doesn't mean anything.

The practitioner is only an improved state of human consciousness; and unless he is watchful, the practitioner is liable to handle a patient with sin and disease. Wouldn't it be better to handle the sin and disease without the patient — impersonally? Because the disease or sin is an error, it doesn't belong to anybody. It is utterly without being, without space or occupancy, without substance, without mind, and without action. It is but a belief in mortal mind, and mortal mind is no mind at all. If the belief or claim of disease is wholly a belief, then it is not a patient or a person. You *must* handle that claim and help that person, but you cannot give a treatment that is so impersonal that it merely floats into space.

The object of a treatment is to handle a specific claim for someone who has called upon you to do so; but you must not keep the patient in the claim or associated with the claim, for the more you can disassociate the claim from the patient, the more dominion you will have, and the more harmony in your own life, simply because you see it wholly as a belief without a believer, without personality, without mind, law or reality.

There is a correct way to approach your work, and not to be too set or too uncertain in the way of treating; and this will require a certain amount of intelligence and demonstration on the part of the practitioner. You will have to attain the very highest understanding to work from, and you must be sure that there is no error that shall elude your vigilance and ability to take care of it.

You take the place of Truth in the case; and it is just as though you were Truth; consequently you handle the error with the light that is in you, and *is* you; and you can always do it. The more spontaneous your thought, the more effective, since it comes from Principle. Your treatment must constantly rise higher to a fuller consciousness of power and strength. Nothing more is required than to know the Truth, and to know it without effort — the treatment rests in action.

Handle the thought of relapse thus: There is no relapse in Mind, no reversal in Mind; and this fact is law to this treatment, a law that sustains and gives this treatment power and presence, dominion and effect. It sustains and maintains that effect without reversal. Truth cannot be reversed, and this treatment cannot be reversed by any argument or suggestion of mental malpractice. It is maintained in Truth, by Truth, as Truth, and its effect or result cannot be reversed in Truth, in belief, or *at all.*

Never take a case feeling that you have something to heal; never tell the patient that you should have been called sooner. "Now is come salvation," means that now is the time to heal. Salvation means nothing but enlightenment. In resolving things into thoughts, do not stop with the thoughts, for the thoughts or beliefs are not any better than the things.

When you are talking to a patient, do not talk over his head. Talk to him in a simple way so that he will understand. You talk to him right where he is in belief; but you treat him right where he is in Truth. In treating children, always take care of the parents. The fear of the parents is about the first thing you will need to handle. Father-Mother God is the only Parent. Always consider children's diseases as urgent; be super-diligent and thorough in children's cases. Children's cases come more or less under medical law.

There is a tendency in bringing up children in Christian Science to let them slide along and just ask for help at the time there is anything the matter with them. Get them to help themselves with their problems. The child needs to assume some responsibility and to be able to stand on his own feet.

Parents and guardians should begin with themselves. They should discipline themselves first. They should gain some dominion over themselves before they attempt to discipline the child. A child's demonstration is often delayed by the parents own disposition. The parent's fear is not the only shortcoming you might have to handle.

Things to Handle When Necessary

1. That man is not one with Principle. Man *is* one with Principle.

2. Handle fear by knowing the all-presence of divine Love.

118

3. Handle pain. The medical law says pain is symptom.

4. Domination of one person by another. This belief covers a multitude of cases. If you visited the home, you might not be able to see it; it might be a very sweet tongue and still be diabolical. You always have Mind to fall back on in cases of domination.

5. Growth on the body is a belief of accretion. A growth cannot develop because creation is complete.

6. Insanity. Divine Mind is his mind and remains perfect. If your patient is in an asylum, handle drugs. The practitioner is to know the power of God.

7. Incurable diseases. Don't classify disease as more or less incurable.
Science and Health 369: 16-22

8. Slow healing. Know that Truth operates immediately. In every treatment handle the claim that another treatment is necessary. If either practitioner or patient believes that another treatment is necessary, the mental reservation will perpetuate the claim.

9. The belief that the patient will pass on. The person may believe that spiritualism is taking him on. Sometimes patients believe they can see a beckoning hand. Handle this belief of suicide. Handle the belief of poison — animal, vegetable, mineral or germ. Realize there are no poisons.

10. Liability to colds and hay-fever. Just realize there is nothing to cause fear or irritation in Truth. There is one substance which is harmonious, never irritated, inflamed or congested — a perfect membrane. It is a claim of hypnotism wholly, also a belief of nerves. Animal magnetism or malpractice of any kind cannot arouse or perpetuate any mental picture of disease or distress.

11. In hay-fever handle everything: fear, membrane, fever, irritation, as mental picture. Always handle superstition with this claim.

12. Injustice. God's government is absolutely just.

13. Opposition to Christian Science by relatives or community. There is no opposition to Truth anywhere, so go fearlessly forward.

14. Discord in Branch Church. Hold to Principle and express more love yourself.

15. Lust. It may be that malpractice is back of it.

16. Paralysis. This might be a stage of venereal disease. If you can destroy fear by putting Love in its place, you will meet paralysis. With paralysis, deny sin absolutely. Go way back and clear it up. Old theology will keep it going.

17. Epilepsy. Sometimes sensuality and sometimes a bad digestive system.

18. Accident. Sometimes people have averted accidents by getting a premonition. Know what might happen and don't let it happen. There must be an alert thought. *Science and Health* 424:5

19. The Claims of Error. Evil claims to exist, to will, to be, to do, to have presence, to have expression, to be a place or a thing. It claims to exist through law, rule, will-power, or wish. Evil should cease from lack of witness. There is no person, place or thing through which evil can act. There is neither an animate or inanimate victim. *Miscellaneous Writings* 67:13-18

20. Medical Records of Disease. Error has no history. Whatever rehearses error is making itself an agent of evil. God has no record of evil or error. Never ask your patient the history of a physical claim. *Message for 1902* 17:17-19.

21. General Malpractice:

The claim that Christian Science does not heal may be ignorant or may be malicious malpractice. The ignorant person says that Christian Science does not heal without any animosity at all. Then there is the malicious type who says it; possibly Roman Catholicism.

The claim that I cannot demonstrate Christian Science, but someone else can. This claim is too big for me; perhaps Mrs. So-and-So had better handle it. Have no doubt about your ability to handle anything.

The claim that I shall not recognize malpractice as such; neither shall I handle it. That old discordant beliefs will return, such as sickness and sin. Know that malpractice cannot produce beliefs.

The claim that there can be a reversal of good plans and desires. Know for each treatment that there can be no reversal.

Other Things to Handle When Necessary

False theology: this has many phases.

Material birth: This has a prominent place in materiality. Get the true sense of pre-existence; the real man never began. We should work for ourselves on pre-existence, that we ourselves existed prior to material birth. The real man was never born; but that doesn't mean we don't love a little child. In true being there is no material birth. A little child is just a belief that life begins. Get your eternal relationship to God, glorifying spiritual existence. Cultivate your spiritual existence.

That we think with brain. *Science and Health* 372:1-13.

That matter is cause. This covers the belief of material pleasure. The belief of material pleasure may be worse than pain. Of course, if Science comes in, that is the end of the belief of pleasure in matter.

Christian Scientists should rid themselves of depraved appetites. Tobacco and alcohol have so much associated with them that is bad.

> *Science and Health* 224:7-8; 405:29-32;
> 406:28-20; 454:1-3
> *Miscellaneous Writings* 240:24-32
> *Miscellany* 106:22-27; 114:3-6.

Sin. Sin is a material belief. All sin is a belief in the reality of matter. Love your neighbor as yourself and do not condemn him.

Heredity. That the good and bad traits of character are handed down from ancestors. Be sure that you handle the good ones too. We are liable to accept the good ones, whereas God is the only ancestor.

Belief that Wrong Measures are Necessary to Success. This needs to be handled. Know that we do not have to resort to *materia medica* or to dishonesty or to unfair methods to succeed.

Luck. Another fallacy. Some people believe luck is against them. There is no element of chance in Principle.

Astrology. *Science and Health* 102:12-15. It is well, under circumstances when things appear to be mysteriously un-lucky and you can't explain it and you work and work on it, to handle the so-called law of astrology. You must know that man was never born into matter, never born under any planetary influence that could influence his life in belief or at all. Then declare: no astrology or horoscope was ever constructed, no chart to outline what man should do. There is no law that can predict, arrange or pre-dictate, for man is governed, controlled and sustained by the divine Mind. Whether a person believes in astrology or not, there is a widespread belief in it; and many doubtless believe in it as just plain superstition.

Palmistry. More mortal illusion and superstition. People have their palms read as a joke; but if they do this, they take something in that is a form of mesmerism.

Theosophy. Theosophy claims to be the wisdom of God. The only wisdom of God is the Truth. It is strongly hypnotic, but is only a phase of mortal mind. *Science and Health* 129:16-20

Destiny. The belief of an evil destiny is linked to fatalism. Evil can produce no effect. God is infinite.

Electricity. There is an educated belief that everything is basically electric. *Science and Health* 93-7-20.

Human Will. Someone extremely willful in a family will sometimes cause much unhappiness. Human will has no place in Christian Science. We have not squared accounts with God if we are harboring evil in any form.

Spiritualism. Primarily, spiritualism is associated with every religious belief in the world except Christian Science. There is not a so-called organized religion in the world that is not more or less spiritualism, because everyone says or assumes that every person has a spirit or soul, and that his spirit or soul goes some-where when he dies. So all of the religious beliefs in the world are more or less spiritualism excepting Christian Science.

The belief of soul in body is spiritualism. The belief that there is communication between the dead and the living is a false claim. Study the chapter on "Spiritualism" in *Science and Health*, and you will understand why there isn't any.

Body

The material concept of body is not body at all. Mrs. Eddy says mortals are material falsities. We become masters of the body in proportion that we see the nothingness of matter. The body is not material; even this body is not material. It is nothing but material beliefs. As a claim, mortal mind claims to be alive in the material body, but there never was a moment when there was any life in a material body. You might take a body apart, and you will not find any life, soul, spirit, or mind; it was never there.

All that influences the human body as thought is outside of it; all fears, superstitions, theories and false beliefs, sins, and diseases are outside of it. You will have to train yourself to shut out these things that claim to govern the body. You are not healing disease; there is no disease to heal. You are healing a belief, and you never treat matter or the material body, so-called. The more clearly you see that it is a condition of thought, and not a condition or matter, the sooner you will master the situation.

We appear to be in a material body, but we are divine embodiment. We think this appearance is our body, yet we are conscious of a lot of things — chairs, tables, books, buildings, people, sunset, stars, the weather — and who shall say that these things that seem to be exterior to us are not a part of our body? They are certainly a part of consciousness, and your consciousness is your body.

There will never be such a thing as the destruction of the body. The thing that we need most to perceive, is that everything that exists, exists spiritually. If you have a body at all, you have a spiritual body.

Rudimental Divine Science 13:6-13.

Nobody can understand about body unless he has advanced understanding of Soul and God, because there is no connection between the human body and the spiritual body or the real man.

What you call the human body is the concept of mortal mind. You must see that everything in matter is unreal. Nobody has a material body. It is untrue that we are looking at each other; we do not exist that way.

The human body is mortal mind; it isn't matter at all. If in your treatment you treat it as matter, you are treating it incorrectly. It is mortal mind; there is nothing to it but belief.

The material body will never be spiritualized; you cannot spiritualize matter. "Matter disappears under the microscope of Spirit." (*Science and Health*) The matter body will never be anything; it isn't anything right now. Matter is only a belief about substance. It does not exist as identity or actuality; it has no being. The only spiritual man is that which you are knowing of God. The thinking is the spiritual man; there is one glorious, immaculate body, expressing dominion and law. Insist upon laying hold of Life eternal, and stop laying hold of those things that constitute nothing but death and age.

When you declare that body is spiritual, you should know that eyes are spiritual, lungs are spiritual, etc., in their true meaning. Do not let the mistaken idea that there is no such thing as eyes in the divine Mind, no such thing as lungs or liver, because if you have one humanly, you have one divinely. And knowing you have one divinely, you will heal the one you have humanly, because the divine fact is the law to the belief, whether of liver or anything else.

Some people are afraid that their denial of the human body will put them out of existence. The East Indians have sometimes denied themselves into a state of unconsciousness that lasts for weeks. We don't want to deny ourselves into unconsciousness. We deny our materiality for the purpose of obtaining true consciousness, and not to put ourselves to sleep.

You should not say, "I deny this whole material existence." That might kill a person. But if you see that his existence is not material, that he is spiritual because God is Spirit, and therefore he cannot be anything but spiritual; all there is to him, even now, is spiritual; and that any appearance to the contrary is a false appearance — that would be a denial of materiality or of material selfhood; but it is the denial arising out of dominion.

A denial in Christian Science is always dominion, and never a fight with matter. If one makes his denial from the standpoint of divine Principle or law, it helps the human body; it frees it and takes away the fear; and if there is anything going wrong, it will have to be right immediately because of that simple fact. It is a mistaken notion to suppose that nothing exists; and it is not right to say there is no body, just as much as it would be to say there is no man. It is never wrong, but always right, to say there is no matter. Get rid of the idea that things don't exist. Everything is — but not material. The claim of separation is the belief that there are many bodies as well as many minds.

The true selfhood that declares its being in Mind, will find the other person in Mind, and that is the one body. The perfect body understood is the absolute healing of every belief about the body without delay or failure. The eternal abiding knowledge of God is your body and my body, and it is wholly well. That which you are conscious of in Truth, is your forever body. The real body and the real man are one. The real man is not an uncertainty, not subject to uncertainty. If you and I apprehend the same idea, that is the same body; and if we apprehend infinite ideas in immeasurable numbers, we have the same body.

What you know and what I know, are all infinite ideas; and we have the satisfaction of knowing that our identity reflects these ideas after its own nature, performing the function of being with certain and unfailing harmony.

The only identity we really have, is understanding; and real being must be understood so that we express our true identity. Identity is a fixed fact in eternity. Ideas can never age or die.

Your own thought that is in accord with God, is your spiritual body, and is more tangible than your appearance. Conscious identity is what you know and not what you seem to be. The real man is unknown to matter, and matter is unknown to him. He is without limitation or time or space; without any sense of coming or going, beginning or ending; without any feeling that he wants something that he cannot have; without any wish or desire that could possibly be otherwise than that which is in consonance with divine Love.

True identity or true individuality will ever be the embodiment of right ideas, infinite, harmonious, and immortal, showing forth their divine nature, expressing good. "The Word will be made flesh and dwell among mortals, only when man reflects God in body as well as in mind." (*Miscellaneous Writings*)

When you see and understand that there is only one I or Us, you will have extraordinary success in your healing work. If one is suffering, tempted, in trouble, or cast down, and one is able to perceive the one body, in that moment there would be relief and complete healing.

The real man is the image or expression of God, Mind, Soul, Life, Truth, and Love, the very expression of infinite Principle of God's own being. This is the only man there is — this is you; this is me; this is everybody; the one and only kind of man, just one. In this sense there is only one man.

The divine Mind is the divine Ego, and the I or Us. We are finding that man *is* man because there is only one Spirit, and that is the only one man has. There is one Soul and that is man's Soul. There is only one Truth, and that is the Truth that is man. There is only one Life, and that is the Life that man has. Man is primarily Mind because there is one Mind and he thinks with it. Man has infinite ideas which declare and reveal an infinite creator, and these are shown forth in individual man; so all there is to him or to his body is the divine Mind.

Man

The moment you understand something of Principle, that understanding is man. As you seek and gain understanding, what you learn is you.

Mrs. Eddy says we know no more of man than we know of God. You have never seen man with your eyes; you will never be able to take cognizance of man by means of the material sense; we cannot find man by searching for man. You only find man by knowing God, the more you know of God, the more you know of man.

For image and likeness, you can substitute the words *evidence* or *expression*. The evidence of God is man. Man is not a thing that reflects God, but is expression; that is quite different. Man is spiritual; he is substance; he is not material; he does not have birth, growth, disintegration, decay or death. He knows none of these things; he has his being in infinity. Get rid of the mental picture of man, and look away from the material man or body. The first, last, and only thing is God. You look into Christian Science and find God. The knowledge or enlightenment is man. When you seek God, you find yourself and others as well.

Man has his being in infinity; he is the expression of Mind and exactly like Mind; therefore man is idea. The divine Mind cannot think of anything different from itself, or contrary to its divine nature. There is distinction between the word *God* and the word *man*, otherwise we would not use both words.

God knows Himself, and the image of Himself is His knowledge of Himself. The moment you understand Spirit, Soul, Mind, Life, Truth, Love, Principle, God, that understanding is the real and only man.

The unfoldment of right ideas which reveal truth is man, constitutes his body or sense of being, which he will have forever.

Revelation is the real man. "The Word was with God." The Word is *man*. All we have to do is awake, become conscious here and now of the divine facts, in order to be all that man is. In the degree that we are awakening through our study, instruction, and demonstration — in that degree we are the divine man. Christian Science is the reflection of the real man.

The material experience is nothing. It is no man. Do not be afraid to declare this and to know it. All there is to man is what he knows. The thing to do is to know that you know, and know that you know it really *is*. Then stand by it. God is omnipresence and intelligence. Man is the perfect idea of God. Divine ideas in their ceaseless and harmonious activity constitute all that man is and all that his body is. The body is not subject to any phase or form of error, or belief of a mind or intelligence apart from God. Man is alert, satisfied, and ever conscious of good. Man is the ceaseless glorification of the infinite Father-Mother God. God is individual and man is the individual expression of God, all harmonious.

The moment that you understand Principle, and it appears to you so real and substantial that you forget you have a belief of material existence, that moment is a foretaste of immortality, and indicates just how immortality will have to be attained. All we have to do is to awake and become conscious here and now of the divine facts of Being in order to be all of what man is. Your thoughts about man will do no good until you see perfection and maintain it.

No two individuals do the same things in the same way, and still both may be right. That is as it should be; there must be individuality. Your individuality is what you know of God as Mind. What you have been able to consciously discern of the knowledge of God — that is you.

The term man is used to designate an infinite idea of the infinite Mind. This idea is a sublime reality. The real man is a state of self-knowledge, reflecting the divine consciousness. His knowledge is the man, and what he knows is his body; and if we know enough, the movements now possible to thought would be possible to body. Man is not limited to the movements of corporeality.

Assuming that there is an infinite cause, you will have to assume an infinite effect. Man is the image of omniscience; he knows everything. He does not have to learn anything; and if we understand that, we will immediately become more spontaneous and secure in our thinking. Man is the expression or evidence of the supreme, all-inclusive consciousness we call God. Mortal sense is the deflection of being, misrepresenting man, who is the reflection. Man is power expressed; not man expressing power. Man is life expressed, and the expression of Life never dies. God is all there is to man. Man is the consciousness, the evidence of the possession of every eternal quality of God.

> *Retrospection and Introspection* 73:6-8
> *No and Yes* 11:5-7
> *Miscellaneous Writings* 79:5-19
> *Science and Health* 258:13-18; 506: 10-14; 477:20-25

We cannot ignore the beliefs that are incidental to human existence. They are often looked upon with too much severity. This is not the way of salvation; the way of salvation is Science. These beliefs are not to be overcome by condemnation or severity of thought. The creation of mortal mind is nothing but separation. The only constant thing about the human being is his desire for completeness. Science, which shows what man really is, shows that he is already complete, satisfied, that he consists of all the qualities that constitute completeness; and reflecting them more and more, he is glorified understanding.

Generic Man

What is generic man, and in what respect does he differ from individual man? The question, by implication, can be called philosophical rather than scientific, for a person could do good work without being able to answer that question satisfactorily. In fact, thousands of practitioners are in that position, and to many the question is far too intellectual to permit of deep consideration. To others it appears to be a rhetorical question, and to some extent not essential. However, ultimately, every Christian Scientist will demonstrate the one Mind so clearly that he will know unmistakably both the likeness and the difference between individual and generic man. As a matter of fact, we ourselves illustrate both. We are individual and yet as one Mind.

We are here collectively or generically as one Mind. Jesus said, "Where two or three (or thirty) are gathered together in my name, there am I in the midst of them." The demonstration of Truth individually illustrates individual man; the demonstration of Truth collectively illustrates generic man. The term *generic man* may be applied to the individual, in a way, because individual consciousness is the likeness of the all-inclusive divine consciousness. To see that the term generic, in the sense of inclusiveness, applies to individual man as well as to universal man, increases one's ability to deal with questions of general or universal import. To state it again: the term *generic* in the sense of inclusiveness, applies to individual man as well as to the universal man. To see that makes us think in a better way.

It expands consciousness to see that man is not confined to anything, has no limitation, cannot limit himself, cannot limit his thought, his power, his action, or his being. He is inclusive of here and there, of what and where and when, and that is the only man there is. *Think that out.*

The recognition of divine relationship and the co-relationship of all ideas is important. The divine man, the only man, generic and individual, forever born, is the unfoldment of ideas. Each individual is but a concrete exemplification of that infinite idea we call generic man. Think that out, too. Generic man is the ideal of infinite Mind, Principle, Love, Spirit, forever unfolding more and more to His creation; and all of this is individually expressed. All the identities we call man are included in the term generic man. The term *generic man* is an individual expression of infinity. "Mind, not matter, is the creator. Love, the divine Principle, is the Father and Mother of the universe, including man." (*Science and Health*)

When Love, the divine Principle, is recognized as the Father-Mother of the universe it will mean the unity and completeness of all being, and of every individual expression of being in the universe. Nothing is more important than to understand this inspiring fact, for the Science of Being rests upon our recognizing the completeness and fullness of what Mrs. Eddy defines in the words: "There is but one I or Us, but one divine Principle, or Mind, governing all existence." (*Science and Health*)

As this divine Principle is infinite, it is always *one*. Its characteristics must necessarily be always infinite and infinitely glorious. One Father-Mother — not one father and one mother — but one complete, self-existent entity, infinitely manifested. For the reason that God, divine Principle is one, so are we one; that is, each one of us is one in completeness and perfection; and taken all together we are one in Principle. Therefore we are one individually and one generically.   The individual man can have no restriction of intelligence or life or love or opportunity or anything else; and all individuals express and represent the ideal of infinite Mind.

It is essential to establish the right idea of God as the real man; and essential to see that the individuality of God has to have infinite expression; therefore you have infinite individuals. I am not a corporeal individual, but an infinite individual.

Complete possession characterizes the real man, the divine man who includes the universe, reflecting the infinite One. Identity is the reflection of Spirit. "God is individual, and man is His individualized idea." (*No and Yes*)

This means that divine individuality is infinitely individualized. The divine Mind, Father-Mother God, is infinite oneness, and individual man is the exact likeness or expression of the oneness, embodying in individuality the infinite ideas, male and female, companionship, and complete satisfaction. These particular metaphysical points are not doctrinal, but fundamental; and an understanding of them is essential to our progress.

Science and Health 515:21-22; 475:14-18

Man expresses all of the eternal qualities of God. Man is not corporeal. God has not one material quality; therefore man cannot reflect matter or materiality. The divine qualities expressed in spiritual man cannot be lost or impaired, because being spiritual and God-given, they remain perfect and indestructible throughout all time. It follows inevitably that man includes all that can properly be meant by the words *sons* and *daughters*, and *male* and *female*; or what would ordinarily be called men and women.

Principle expresses itself in ideas; and there is no other possible expression of Principle except ideas; therefore when Mrs. Eddy speaks of men and women in Science, she speaks of them as ideas. She doesn't anywhere speak of male and female as separate individuals going on forever; that would not be Christian Science. Principle, God, is infinite and therefore one; for this reason man is not two — not a male and a female — but is   one; and he is the exact likeness of God. So in Christian Science, companionship between male and female is satisfactory in proportion to its true oneness, or blending of ideas in spiritual unity.

Mrs. Eddy had a broad outlook, organizing ability and courage, which were   supposed to be male characteristics; but with her, they were distinct ideas and did not touch her appearance or manner. There never was a more womanly woman. So man should, and in reality does, have all the gentleness and tenderness that is supposed to belong to a woman.

We are not like one another; we are individuals like Mind, like infinity. We cannot lose nor lack this spiritual completeness. We must claim it and express it individually, and thus embody all right ideas. God being *one*, the image and likeness of God is never two separate bodies, but one — one being, one individuality. Don't fear that you are going to lose something or lack something, or that in some way or other if you find your completeness, you won't be satisfied. If you have always wanted your completeness, you will find complete associations, and in this completeness you will find that which we call association here. We are one wonderful body — this class — showing forth the infinity of one infinite Mind.

God is Mind, and Mind finds expression in idea and *as* idea, and never in any other way. Therefore we can say that God's all-inclusive conscious expression is a compound idea embracing all right ideas. This compound idea has no limit to being, individually or collectively. Infinity could never conceive of anything finite, therefore every idea is an infinite idea.

Generic man has been described as the sum total of right ideas, but that definition is not correct, for there is no sum total to infinity. "Creation is ever appearing and must ever continue to appear from the nature of its inexhaustible source." (*Science and Health*). There is no sum total here.

When man is depicted as material and mortal, Science affirms and confirms his identity as spiritual and eternal. Generic man is humanly represented as mankind; perhaps it would be more accurate to say misrepresented. Mankind is a term which in the last analysis dignifies human consciousness, universal human consciousness. Who could imagine all that this term implies? And who, with any understanding of Christian Science, would want to imagine this false consciousness? Nevertheless, when we consider that all the instances, circumstances, and events that make up history, as well as the possibilities of history — error — that have not yet appeared, constitute mortal mind and its generic representative, mankind, we can understand something of the magnitude of the term *mankind*; boundless as the meaning is to finite sense, it is but a finite or false sense and statement concerning generic man. A true concept of generic man is essential to our individual progress. There is nothing in or to generic man that is impossible to individual man. The infinite generic idea is also the infinite individual idea.

Consciousness includes all ideas without limitation of distance or time. The infinite idea of infinite Mind includes all individuality, is generic man. God is infinite, and God is Mind. The image and likeness of God is, and must be, an infinite spiritual idea capable of division and subdivision into an infinity of lesser ideas. Generic man finds expression in individual man.

The infinite idea of infinite Mind, including all individuality, is what you will have to see and understand as the only possible entity that can express God. Generically and individually man is infinite. Every individual idea is infinite. Consciousness expresses itself as individual as well as generic man. Consciousness is the basic and primal fact of all being. All that means infinite male and female is found in the words, Father-Mother Mind.

Science and Health 586:9 (to second;); 592:16-17

These infinite qualities, indicated in the above references, blend into one entity, one being. Every individual is the reflection of Father-Mother. He is not a state of longing, consciously or unconsciously. He is a state of completeness wherein there is no matter, and hence no desire, no want, no longing — just the unfoldment of infinite ideas, ever appearing, ever glorifying and praising God, all reflected in individual man.

Generic man is an expression comprising all individuals. It is divine individuality, infinity individualized. Generic man is the infinity of all of the ideas of Mind, the one infinite intelligence, expressed in multitudinous ideas, which are forever unfolding from the boundless basis of infinite Principle. In this way, man is the full representation of Mind.

Generic Man, creation, and the universe are synonymous terms. Generic man is the universe, and includes the universe. The universe includes individual man, and the individual man includes the universe. It is all in man; it is all in consciousness. Generic man is the infinite individuality of individual man; infinite and divinely

135

individualized. Man is the perfect and complete expression of Father-Mother God, a state of sublime, conscious completeness and harmonious being. Generic man is an expression comprising all individuality. This expression of Mind and its immediate ideas, this real man who is appearing never to disappear, is ourselves. It is your identity, my identity, our identity.

The term *man* includes all that is called mankind. Man means all men and every creature individually, wanting nothing to beautify, glorify, or purify his existence. Co-existent with God, he has eternal life and indestructible substance. He possesses in infinite measure every quality that makes his creator harmonious, invincible and supreme. Man is so like God that there are no means possible for separation. As expression, man is a state of complete possession. He is complete in every step of his being, and as a divine idea represents Father-Mother Mind. His characteristics are love, harmony, dominion, accomplishment, clear discernment, perfect and accurate action in everything that he thinks, says or does.

Man and his activities are absolutely impervious to any influence other than that of infinite divine Principle, supreme Mind, of which he is the full and inevitable expression, incapable of even the slightest variation from absolute perfection. Being the perfect idea of infinite Mind, man has within himself all that constitutes complete and harmonious being. He lacks nothing; he does not desire; he is possession.

When you gain the true concept of God as Mind, you will realize God's availability and that you are *always* in His presence. Isn't intelligence always available? Nothing can separate you from intelligence. "God is not separate from the wisdom He bestows." (*Science and Health*) God's intelligence is your intelligence. Your true self is God's expression. His life is your life. His being is your being. Man is the manifested presence or expression of infinite good. He is spiritual and perfect; he is the embodiment of all right ideas, the direct expression of infinite Mind. He is at one with and inseparable from divine Mind.

Omnipresent Love supplies man's every need and keeps him in his perfect place and position forever. As a divine idea in the consciousness of Mind, he is as eternal and indestructible as Truth itself. He is never born and never dies. Man is not subject to matter; he does not live in matter, on matter, nor because of matter; nor is he subject to any beliefs of mortal mind. He is perfect and complete in every phase of his being, and cannot be touched by chance, lack, loss or accident. As the full expression of his Maker, man is conscious only of harmony, dominion, and abundance.

"If there arise a matter too hard for thee in judgment, between blood and blood, between plea and plea, and between stroke and stroke, being matters of controversy within my gates: then shalt thou arise, and get thee up into the place which the Lord thy God shall chose." "Ye shall not respect persons in judgment; but ye shall hear the small as well as the great; ye shall not be afraid of the face of man; for the judgment is God's: and the cause that is too hard for you, bring it unto me, and I will hear it."(Deut. 17: 8; 1:7)

Whatever Truth comes to you, you are hearing the voice of Principle. Whenever Truth comes to you, you are hearing the voice of Principle.

For further information regarding Christian Science:
Write: The Bookmark
          Post Office Box 801143
          Santa Clarita, CA 91380
Call: 1-800-220-7767
Visit our website: www. thebookmark.com

ABOUT THE AUTHOR: Bicknell Young was born in Salt Lake City, Utah, in 1856 — the youngest of eleven children. His father, Joseph Young, was a brother of Brigham Young, and his family was prominent in the Mormon Church.

As a boy, Bicknell Young was a brilliant student. He was also gifted with a beautiful voice and a natural talent for music. He studied voice and piano with the best teachers in Salt Lake City, before traveling abroad to study. In 1879, he was granted admission to the National School of Music and then the Royal College of Music, both in London, England. While at the Royal College, he met Eliza Mazzucato. After Mr. Young completed his training, he and Elisa were married. They later had three sons.

Mr. and Mrs. Young left England in 1885 to open a music school in Salt Lake City. Their talents brought unusual style and grace to Salt Lake City. But despite the adulation of the music patrons there, the couple moved to Omaha, Nebraska, and then, in 1890, to Chicago, Illinois.

Shortly after arriving in Chicago, Mr. Young became gravely ill. When the doctors were unable to help him, someone referred him to a Christian Science practitioner, and he was completely healed. As a result, Mr. and Mrs. Young took up the study of Christian Science and joined the Church. In 1895, the Youngs had Primary Class with Edward Kimball, and Mr. Young was appointed Committee on Publication for Illinois. In 1901, they attended Mr. Kimball's Normal Class and Mr. Young became a teacher. During the 1890s, his mother and many of his sisters and relatives were converted to Christian Science. His mother was a member of his first class.

In 1903, he was appointed to the Board of Lectureship. From then until 1928 Mr. Young lectured throughout the world, except for the three years when he was First Reader of The Mother Church (1917-1920). Mr. Young lectured in the Albert Hall in London to 9,900 people. He was the first lecturer to make a round-the-world tour.

In 1909 Mrs. Eddy requested the Youngs to take up residence in England, and they remained there for four years, visiting every church and society in the European Field. He returned briefly to Boston to teach the Normal Class of 1910. In 1937 he again taught the Normal Class. At the time of his passing in 1938, he was known as the "Dean of Christian Science Teachers."

138

the advent of euo

self - will
self - just forte ⇒ we're not here
self - love   to do anyo
                              we're
                          excu me

I'm work art
to think/are to be love
— to never get people stuck — lily
          people been feel - deserve —
          lily people helps
how to heel — hurt to heal
          use trapped — been the prayer
grey — nothing can affect me
but that God is the only cause —
there is nothing out the true so —
I can't take the stone
its because I'm body at the body
age is a lot)
     it can't inhent it — don't feel
          overwhelm you it a treated
but we believe there. can
          take arm m life, we
don't look for the physical heal to
          verify — inside also I know
          to be true
     — work in the stay that is
don't cut the body been my God